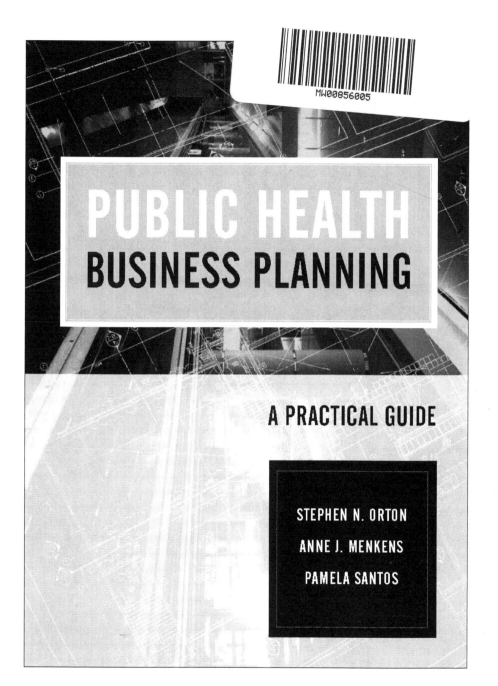

PUBLIC HEALTH
BUSINESS PLANNING

A PRACTICAL GUIDE

STEPHEN N. ORTON

ANNE J. MENKENS

PAMELA SANTOS

JONES AND BARTLETT PUBLISHERS
Sudbury, Massachusetts
BOSTON   TORONTO   LONDON   SINGAPORE

World Headquarters

Jones and Bartlett Publishers
40 Tall Pine Drive
Sudbury, MA 01776
978-443-5000
info@jbpub.com
www.jbpub.com

Jones and Bartlett Publishers
Canada
6339 Ormindale Way
Mississauga, Ontario L5V 1J2
Canada

Jones and Bartlett Publishers
International
Barb House, Barb Mews
London W6 7PA
United Kingdom

Jones and Bartlett's books and products are available through most bookstores and online booksellers. To contact Jones and Bartlett Publishers directly, call 800-832-0034, fax 978-443-8000, or visit our website www.jbpub.com.

Substantial discounts on bulk quantities of Jones and Bartlett's publications are available to corporations, professional associations, and other qualified organizations. For details and specific discount information, contact the special sales department at Jones and Bartlett via the above contact information or send an email to specialsales@jbpub.com.

This publication is designed to provide accurate and authoritative information in regard to the Subject Matter covered. It is sold with the understanding that the publisher is not engaged in rendering legal, accounting, or other professional service. If legal advice or other expert assistance is required, the service of a competent professional person should be sought.

Production Credits
Publisher: Michael Brown
Associate Editor: Katey Birtcher
Production Editor: Rachel Rossi
Marketing Manager: Sophie H. Fleck
Manufacturing and Inventory Control Supervisor: Amy Bacus
Composition: Paw Print Media
Cover Design: Brian Moore
Printing and Binding: Malloy, Inc.
Cover Printing: Malloy, Inc.

ISBN: 978-1-4496-4350-8

Library of Congress Cataloging-in-Publication Data
Orton, Stephen Noyes.
   Public health business planning : a practical guide / Stephen N. Orton, Anne J. Menkens, Pamela Santos.
      p. ; cm.
   Includes bibliographical references.
   ISBN-13: 978-0-7637-4621-6
   ISBN-10: 0-7637-4621-5
   1. Public health administration. 2. Community health services—Planning. 3. Health planning. 4. Business planning. I. Menkens, Anne J. II. Santos, Pamela. III. Title.
   [DNLM: 1. Community Health Planning—United States. 2. Public Health Administration—economics—United States. 3. Marketing of Health Services—United States. 4. Models, Organizational—United States. WA 546 AA1 O78p 2009]
   RA425.O57 2009
   362.1068—dc22
                                        2007050235
   6048

Printed in the United States of America
15 14 13   10 9 8 7 6 5 4 3

Dedication

To our families, whose love and patient support are ever-sustaining.

Give me six hours to chop down a tree and I will spend the first four sharpening the axe.
—Abraham Lincoln

Contents

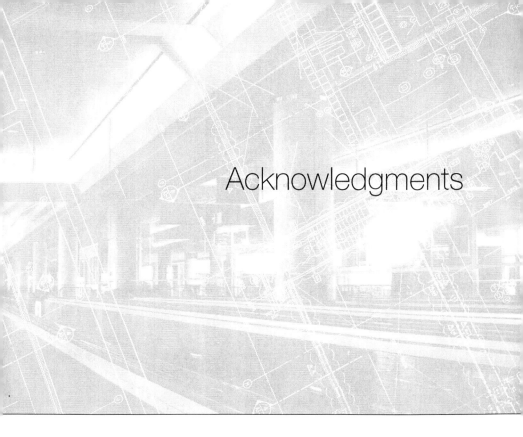

Acknowledgments

The proper acknowledgment of everyone who made this book possible might be longer than the book. It would include the nearly 900 graduates of the Management Academy for Public Health who have come to our program and put their sweat equity into producing business plans to fulfill course requirements, then gone home and tried to implement those plans. They did the work: we just took notes. We read their business plans and copied out the parts that illustrated best practices for different sections. We checked up with them to ask: How are you doing? Why is it working? What barriers are you encountering? How would you do it differently next time? They have all been, without fail, gracious and generous with their time. Even if their plan doesn't appear in the book, we thank all graduates for what they have lent to our understanding of public health business planning.

Several individuals who either attended the Management Academy, or have been responsible for sending teams over the years, read early drafts and helped us revise and stay relevant. Especially helpful were Beth Lovette, Anne Thomas, and Dorothy Cumbey, who each responded with thoughtful comments that, we believe, strengthened the usefulness of our book for our primary audience of managers in governmental public health settings.

For individual chapters, special thanks goes to Management Academy alumni Carl Humphries, CEO, and Derek Brown, Director of Development and QI, of HopeHealth in South Carolina, who shared their story with us for Chapter 14. Mary Davis, Director of Evaluation Services at the NC Institute for Public Health, made very helpful suggestions and contributions to Chapter 10, on evaluation, and John Dreyzehner's thoughts and experiences contributed to our discussion of the broad benefits of partnering, found in Chapter 7. Many excellent staff and coaches helped shape the business plan projects we describe throughout, especially business plan coach Catherine McClain. Finally, thanks to evaluator Karl Umble and his many graduate assistants, whose work gathering and analyzing outcomes data informed our "What Can Go Wrong" sections for every chapter, as well as discussion related to outcomes throughout the book.

Lloyd Novick and Jan Carney provided extremely thoughtful and helpful reviews of our manuscript, and Mike Brown and Katey Birtcher at Jones and Bartlett have been responsive and supportive throughout.

Beyond these immediate impacts, this book is entirely dependent on the vision and hard work of many people who preceded us in imagining and designing the Management Academy. Four founding organizations came together in 1999 to create the idea and fund the Management Academy: The Centers for Disease Control and Prevention, the Health Resources and Services Administration, the W. K. Kellogg Foundation, and the Robert Wood Johnson Foundation, assisted by the CDC Foundation. Individuals who advised those organizations and have worked over the years since then to ensure that the program would be successful include Barbara Sabol, Sue Hassmiller, Tom Balderson, Martha Katz, Earl Fox, Charlie Stokes, and Richard House. Ed Baker has helped all along the way, at CDC at the very beginning up until today as director of the NC Institute for Public Health. These individuals' contributions to the success of this program cannot be overstated.

We would like to acknowledge the North Carolina Institute for Public Health for providing institutional support during the writing of this manuscript. This publication was also supported in part by a grant from the W. K. Kellogg Foundation (P0110066). The contents are solely the responsibility of the authors and do not necessarily represent the official views of the Institute or the Kellogg Foundation.

And finally, every good idea about business planning and sustainable enterprise in this book can be traced back to the wisdom, generosity, and committed action of Jim Johnson at the Kenan-Flagler Business School, the original co-director of the Management Academy, and Janet Porter, the other founding co-director of the Management Academy and now COO of the Dana-Farber Cancer Institute. They inspired this book, in every sense. To the extent that you hear their voices, we consider this book a success. Thank you.

About the Authors

Stephen Orton is Deputy Director of the Office of Executive Education at the North Carolina Institute for Public Health, the service and outreach arm of the School of Public Health. Dr. Orton also holds an Adjunct Assistant Professor appointment in the Health Policy and Administration Department. He has worked in public health executive education since 1994; he was the first program manager for the Management Academy for Public Health, in 1999. He earned his PhD in English from UNC-Chapel Hill in 1998.

Anne Menkens is a Program Director at the North Carolina Institute for Public Health Office of Executive Education. She has worked in public health education and research communications since 1997 and is responsible for the planning and implementation of Executive Education Alumni programs as well as writing and editing projects for the Institute. She earned her MA in English from the University of North Carolina at Chapel Hill and is currently pursuing a PhD.

Pamela Santos is a Business Plan Advisor for the Management Academy for Public Health. She is also Senior Management Consultant with the Urban Investment Strategies Center in the Kenan Institute of Private Enterprise at the University of North Carolina at Chapel Hill. In this role, she works with nonprofit organizations and communities to develop income-generating strategies to become more sustainable and competitive in today's knowledge-based economy. Ms. Santos has an MBA from the University of North Carolina-Chapel Hill. She earned a bachelor's degree in Management and Marketing from the University of North Carolina-Greensboro.

Prefaces

I. Making Things Happen

Public health managers and leaders have dreams, bold ideas about ways they could improve the health of the communities they serve. But many times these bold dreams are just that—dreams. They never materialize. There are many reasons for this—lack of resources, lack of political support, regulatory barriers. But perhaps the greatest barrier is public health managers' lack of execution skills; the inability to turn fantasies into reality.

We in public health like to think that this is because of the multi-disciplinary nature of the field with health departments being led by those trained as epidemiologists or nutritionists or those who majored in health and human behavior. None of their training covers even the most basic management skills.

However, the interesting thing is that this skills deficit is not just in public health. It is rampant in business too. A few years ago *Fortune* magazine had a cover story entitled "Why Leaders Fail," referring to leaders of Fortune 500 companies. The article went on to say that failure stems not from lack of vision or great ideas, but the inability to execute those ideas. The ability to make new things happen—to develop a new program, to expand services, to partner with community organizations, to impact health status—is what distinguishes average public health managers from outstanding public health managers. For it is not managing the status quo but rather reaching out to develop new sustainable programs that leaves an imprint on the community.

When diagnosing the contributing factors to the inability to execute, many ideas come to mind—many of which are considered outside the control of public health. But one major factor is the inability to develop a public health business plan. What does a business plan do? It conveys a compelling argument to key stakeholders that a new program or service or expansion will be a sustainable model for addressing a problem. What makes the argument compelling? A clear statement of the community need and a thorough explanation of how the new initiative will address that need. The use of models from similar programs that have worked in other communities. (This is in keeping with General Electric's motto, "Stolen with Pride.") A clear financial plan that illustrates financial sustainability over time. These are just some of the elements of a successful business plan.

What we have learned from the managers attending the Management Academy for Public Health is how gratifying it is for those who have long held their dreams at bay to light up, to be energized, at the notion that their ideas can become reality. Because we are all drawn to public health because we want to make a difference, learning to write a compelling business plan is the means to that end.

Janet E. Porter, PhD
Executive Vice President & Chief Operating Officer
Dana-Farber Cancer Institute

II.

Public health services are delivered through a mix of governmental, not-for-profit, and private partnerships aligned in the interests of promoting and protecting health. The traditional functions of public health—assessment, policy development, and assurance—are well understood by public health practitioners. Less familiar, but growing in understanding and appreciation, is the application of business efficiency and accountability tools to public health practices.

Nowadays, the knowledge and skills of business are as important to public health practice as the skills of the statistician, health educator, and sanitarian. Finding efficiencies in the face of flat or reduced funding streams, modeling accountability in times of increased expectations, and marketing health messages to diverse and media-savvy audiences are but a few of the opportunities for application of sound business practices.

This book, *Public Health Business Planning: A Practical Guide*, should become required reading for both the novice and experienced public health professional. Overall, the book lays out a comprehensive justification for a "public health business plan" and each chapter provides a clear and thorough review of the necessary components of such a plan.

Taking the time to consider and apply the approaches outlined in this book will better prepare today's public health practitioner for tomorrow's public health challenges.

Paul Jarris, MD, MBA
Executive Director
Association of State and Territorial Health Officials

III.

The National Association of County and City Health Officials (NACCHO) is pleased to have an opportunity to recommend *Public Health Business Planning: A Practical Guide*. NACCHO is the national organization representing local governmental public health departments. As such, we work to support efforts that protect and improve the health of all people and all communities by promoting national policy, developing resources and programs, seeking health equity, and supporting effective local public health practice and systems. We support collaboration with the entire public health system, which includes state and federal organizations, as well as other public and private organizations in their communities, state, and nation.

Surely Lewis Carroll was correct when he said, "If you don't know where you are going, any road will get you there." Not having a plan can end up with an organization making many costly mistakes, dealing with the fallout from a failed project, or producing an end result that does not meet its original objectives. For local health departments this can also mean a loss of credibility and even trust from the community at large and elected officials. There are times when we really don't have the luxury of learning from our mistakes.

We all inherently know that having a well thought out, flexible plan helps guarantee success and sustainability of the work we do, especially when that work involves the engagement of different parties and sectors. Planning, however, takes time and commitment. Often we feel we have too little time and that our commitment needs to be demonstrated by taking action. Therefore, we're often tempted to jump into starting a project without thinking about all of its components, the different roles that need to be fulfilled, the requirements that must be addressed prior to, during, and in follow-up to the project, and very importantly, the costs. This book demystifies the planning process by explaining each component and what needs to be considered. When completed, you will have a business plan that either encourages you to continue on your path or to make adjustments to end up where you want to be.

We are told and we tell ourselves, we in public health need to be risk takers. But I think the risks we need to embrace are more about what we undertake than how we do it. In fact, solid planning is a key in managing the risk and ensuring success. Public health today is constantly evolving—it's complex and fast-paced. But that's not really all that different from other sectors as well. We need to take the concepts developed in those other sectors that have enabled them to succeed, such as business, communications, and informatics, and mold them to our needs.

Patrick M. Libbey
Executive Director
National Association of County and City Health Officials
July 2007

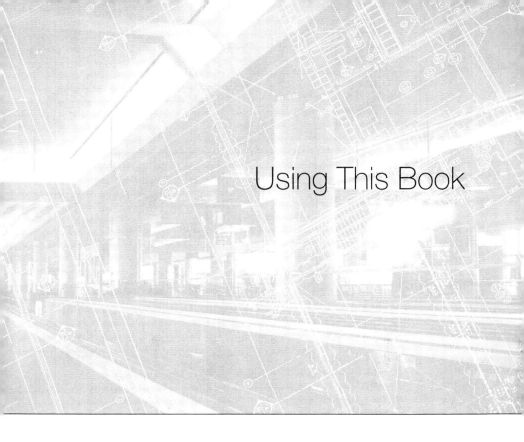

Using This Book

There are books about business planning, and books about public health, but we have put the two together around a very concrete task: writing a business plan for a program intended to address a public health challenge. That's it. We define terms and refer to a few outside references, but most of this book is a how-to guide for writing the plan that will help you get your work done.

This book presents lessons from the Management Academy for Public Health (www.maph.unc.edu), a mid-career training program for public health managers that combines a business education with a public health focus, run jointly by the University of North Carolina School of Public Health and the UNC Kenan-Flagler Business School. The capstone project of the program is a business plan each team creates to address a public health challenge in their communities, a plan they expect to implement after the program. We've had over 900 participants in the program since its inception in 1999: so we have a lot of lessons to draw on.

The primary audience for our program, the audience we know best, is made up of public health practitioners. If this is you, these are our suggestions for using this book:

1. Skim the book from start to finish to get a feel for the whole process, and read the first chapters to understand what we mean by "business planning in public health."
2. Read Chapter 3 to see what the parts of your finished plan will look like.
3. Read the following chapters, which define each of these parts in more detail, give examples, and explain "What Can Go Wrong" (and what to do about it).
4. Decide on an initiative that fits within your organizational goals and is appropriate for a business plan (involves revenue generation, involves partners, is reasonable). Consider the questions that end each chapter. Jot down answers, where you'll find answers, or who you'll assign to get the answers. Jot down more questions. Go to our website (www.publichealthbusinessplanning.org) to explore the topic further.
5. When you've read the whole book, go back and begin answering in detail the questions that end each chapter. Form a committee. Call in partners. Ask a business manager to join the team. Put on a pot of coffee—you have work to do.

If you're still a student, read the book to understand what you may be doing, the challenges you may face, when and if you find yourself in a public health organization. You'll find the "Your Turn" exercises on our web site (http://www.publichealthbusinessplanning.org) especially good for helping you begin the process of thinking and talking about these issues. And, join the Community of Practice blog. We'll be happy to hear from you.

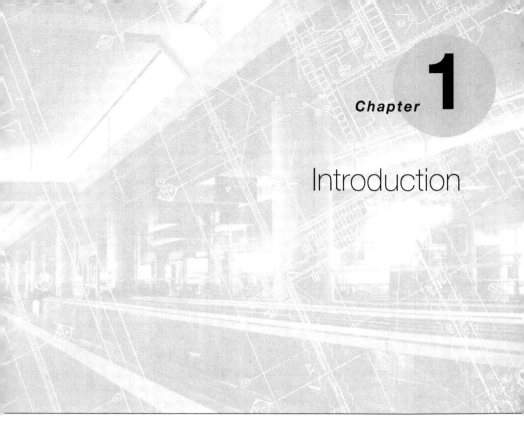

Chapter **1**

Introduction

Why a Business Planning Book?

This book is designed to help you learn a critical skill for success in improving community health: business planning. Most people have a notion of what is meant by a business plan, but many have never written one, or even seen one. Our goal is to demystify the term *business plan* for people like you, doing public health work.

This won't be difficult, for a couple of reasons:

1. Even if you've never seen one, you will recognize virtually every part of the business plan. The models you see in this book will not surprise you. Business plans are designed to answer basic questions that anyone would ask before spending money on a project. What is the need? What is the idea for addressing this need? What is it meant to accomplish? Who is involved? How will it work? Where are the barriers? How much will it cost? The business planning process is, at its best, very practical and accessible; it is designed

1

to analyze and explain a business proposal in terms that an average non-expert can understand.

2. You will find a huge overlap between business planning and the kind of program planning that you do regularly and understand deeply. Terminology is sometimes different, but good program planning shares many traits with good business planning. The differences are instructive, and we will examine them, but often we will highlight similarities.

Who Should Read This Book?

Business planning is a useful and appropriate tool for public health managers at this historical point. If you are like the professionals we have worked with on business planning since 1999—and we've worked with thousands of them in our leadership and management programs—then you already understand how the environment is changing.

The term *public health* is relatively new—within the last century—and the science and practice have moved quickly. Perhaps because the phrase is relatively new, *public health professional* is not a common term; indeed, some people whose work centers on improving the health of populations of people wouldn't define themselves as public health professionals at all. In writing this book, we have in our heads a fairly broad definition of public health professional that includes people in and out of government who take responsibility for some slice of community or population health. They might be working nationally or locally, in a neighborhood or on one street; they might define their "population" in any number of ways: in terms of age (school-age kids) or health risk (asthma sufferers), or location (urban), for instance. The common thread is that they are concerned with groups, not just individuals, and thus take a community view of health and safety.

Clearly this definition includes tens of thousands of people who work in local, state, and federal government. And it clearly includes people in thousands of other organizations—schools, hospitals, nonprofits, and other government agencies such as emergency management or social work—that share concerns and probably have partnerships with health departments.

Health departments today are expected to perform three main tasks: assess the health of the community, ensure that systems are in place to address health problems, and develop policies to promote health and prevent disease. It is clear in the literature and practice of public health over the past several decades that in order to fulfill these expectations, governmental public health workers at all levels depend heavily on a wide network of other organizations—inside and outside the government—to take up a piece of "community health" and become part of the public health "system." Social workers and community organizers take up a piece; administrators in hospitals and schools take up a piece; rural primary care doctors and Indian Health Service administrators take up a piece; developers and corporate leaders and legislators and environmental health inspectors take up a piece. If you are working—or planning to work—in an organization that commits time, money, and energy to creating healthier populations, this book addresses you.

Why Business Planning?

Some have argued that the United States doesn't have a true system for public health. That is a discussion for another day, however. We plan to take the public health environment as we find it. Optimal or not, the current system for preventing disease and promoting health involves a complicated array of organizations, goals, and funding mechanisms. Business planning is a tool that can help public health organizations—and public health partnerships of more than one organization—achieve success in the current environment.

The environment is certainly difficult. Public health organizations today face big challenges in a context of constant change: demographic, economic, geopolitical, and sociocultural trends are transforming American society. James Johnson[1] describes two demographically driven phenomena that suggest what the future will look like. First is the "browning" of America—the increasing role that nonwhite ethnic groups are playing in the growth of the U.S. population. Put simply, increasing diversity means the public health system issues of access and health disparities—already critical problems in many parts of the country—will become even more critical in the coming decades.

Second, Johnson highlights the "graying" of America—the growing share of the population that is 65 or older. This trend means large numbers of Americans are aging out of the labor market, with potentially serious implications for government financing of health care and public health, as well as new challenges that go along with aging, such as chronic disease treatment and prevention, and long-term care issues. And as the population is aging, the birth rate continues to fall among most subgroups. As a country we will have fewer and fewer workers contributing to the support of more and more retirees.

Both trends, "browning" and "graying," raise concerns about the viability of the public health workforce itself, a workforce that in the United States is currently much older and whiter than the population it serves. Some groups, including minority groups and U.S. immigrant populations, are young, with relatively high birth rates, so solutions to the workforce problem are at hand, if we can mobilize them—but new managers will have to be recruited and trained to work in a difficult, rapidly changing public health environment, facing health challenges that are likely to be much more difficult than those of the last century.

The economic environment adds another challenge to the already daunting state of affairs. For a variety of reasons—political, economic, demographic—traditional sources of funding for public health have changed substantially and will almost certainly continue to change. First, government funding at all levels is in decline. The problem is especially acute at the local level, because local public health depends on a mix of federal, state, and county funds—and some jurisdictions in the Northeast add a layer of administration at the township level. A primary implication of these changes is the pressure of accountability on public health managers. After many years of cuts, government budget planners have to make hard choices: not eliminating empty positions but eliminating jobs; not shrinking programs but cutting programs. You may already have experienced this process. If you have, you know the pressure of accounting for every cent you spend. You can reduce the risk of your program's being cut by applying and demonstrating business planning: if you can marshal some combination of outcomes data, critical need (e.g., deep community support or legislative mandate), and ability to generate revenue, you may be able to avoid the "ax."[2]

Second, many foundations have changed the way they make grants. Instead of supporting programs indefinitely, they try to invest strategically in starting up high-quality, high-leverage programs that in a fairly short time frame can become self-sustaining. Public health has many stories of programs that ran to the end of their grant support and then ended. In every case, some community or another loses a (more or less) important service, and staff had to change or lose their jobs. Clearly, these situations help none of the parties: the granting foundation sees no further progress toward its mission, the grantee organization loses funding and perhaps reputation and staff as well, and the community being served generally winds up feeling worse than before. The lack of a service is felt most painfully by those who had it and then lost it, as you know if your cable has ever been disconnected.

In light of these trends, clearly a new way of thinking about developing and sustaining public health initiatives is in order.

Why Now?

Ours is a business-centric culture, and the current cultural moment is especially business-centric (to the extent that the president in power at this writing describes himself as a CEO). Styles change. But the idea that government in general—and public health in particular—might study good businesses to find useful techniques is simply good practice. Success in business requires some skills that are very relevant to public health professionals: listening to constituents, customizing for specific groups, maintaining a satisfied and productive workforce, constantly improving quality, studying the industry, understanding and managing how money flows, forecasting and preparing for things that have not yet happened.

In the 21st century, many successful businesses also have learned to partner, a skill that we've noted is a key success factor for public health professionals. And because many in public health would like to establish partnerships with the business community, a second goal you might have is to understand better how business thinks. The 2003 IOM Report, *The Future of the Public's Health in the 21st Century*,[3] emphasizes that this understanding should go both ways. In making the connection between businesses as employers, and their effect on (and responsibility for) their employees' health, the report suggests that the corporate and governmental public health communities should learn the language of public health, the better to understand their responsibilities and opportunities for improving the community's health.

Getting businesspeople to learn the language of public health, however important, is only half the picture. As Janet Porter has identified,[4] the fundamental element of a sustained partnership is humility. Lacking humility, you will do everything yourself. Partners, by contrast, must believe they need each other to accomplish a goal. You can find corporate partners if you appreciate fully what those partners have—and what you need from them. In turn, tell them what you have to offer that *they* need.

Language is an issue even within public health organizations. Many public health administrative managers who attend our program say that they and their own business managers "speak different languages"—that the administrators have only vague understandings of the budgets their business managers prepare, for example. So, whether we are forming outside partnerships or understanding the workings of our own organizations, understanding "the business of public health" is an important goal.

As a reader of this book, one of your goals might be to "run things more like a business." Of course "running things more like a business" is an oversimplification. As Jim Collins, author of *Good to Great: Why Some Companies Make the Leap...and Others Don't* and *Good to Great and the Social Sectors*, points out,[5] plenty of businesses are poorly run. Of course you don't want to run your agency like a mediocre business. Further, many of us in the government and nonprofit sectors distrust corporate motives generally, and not without reason. Plenty of businesses let the profit motive eclipse more community-conscious motives: they think short term, letting quarterly profits drive decision making; stop at little to wring another drop of margin out of every transaction; treat their employees as expendable commodities. Your goal should be to emulate the best practices of good businesses—and only those practices that are appropriate to the public health enterprise.

Those of us in government are not blameless either. Short-term thinking might sound familiar. Have we ever reorganized to get a three-year grant? Cranked out a grant proposal in under a week? Have we ever scrambled at the end of the fiscal year to spend money before it goes away? Do we have living five-year strategic plans, or are we chasing grants? Perhaps we aren't so different from businesses after all. Whereas businesses at their worst let the profit motive eclipse the good of the community, some of us let our desire to do good for the community eclipse our common sense. We can pride ourselves on not wringing profits out of the community—unless at the same time we're wasting resources because we don't know our costs and don't look for efficiencies. We can pride ourselves on our civic engagement—unless at the same time we're providing communities with programs they don't want, or worse, programs that don't work. We can pride ourselves on giving our employees a venue in which to pursue noble goals—as long as they all understand organizational strategy and objectives, have the resources necessary to do their jobs, feel empowered to make decisions, and feel motivated and appreciated and reasonably well-paid.

What Is a Public Health Business Plan?

A public health business plan is like a private-sector business plan, except that it describes a project to address a public health need rather than a private-sector consumer's need. It is a written document, of approximately 20 pages, that describes and argues for a financially sustainable program in public health. Those 20 pages, broken up into several sections, present both an analysis of the problem and an argument for one way to address it through business-type practices such as establishing partnerships, generating revenue, and establishing measurements for quality control and improvement.

A business plan is not a strategic plan. Strategic plans list priority areas for action. A business plan is instead an analysis of one single project idea (ideally an idea that addresses a priority issue from your existing strategic plan). It offers a detailed recommendation for one specific action. You only need a business plan if your idea is to generate revenue. You would not need a business plan to describe a totally grant- or tax-funded program. You cannot use a business plan for all the things you have to do as a public health manager. You can and should use it for designing a sustainable, revenue-generating program.

At its best, the public health business plan marries a mission to create a healthier community with a long-term strategy for sustainability based on solid analysis. The work is hard, but the steps are not. And the payoffs are great: better planning means better chances for success, in terms of measurable outcomes. In other words, doing more (good) with less (grant funding). This book is designed to help you ensure that you've understood the need, brought the right partners to the table, identified and lined up the necessary resources, and created an effective and efficient blueprint for launching and sustaining a program.

A good business plan is an indispensable guide for a decision maker, but it is also a confirmation to a funder that a program is well planned and well positioned to succeed, and a sea-chart by which a manager can navigate a program through implementation and evaluation. The image of nautical travel highlights a critical point we wish to make: the people and the programs that succeed with this business planning process will combine the flamboyant skills of adventurers on the high seas—speed, strength, flexibility, commitment, leadership— with the reflective skills of careful captains, taking the time to review best practices, select a safe, efficient vessel, study maps, and outfit and staff an expedition appropriately.

When we're not comparing them to seafarers, we call the people who succeed at writing and implementing public health business plans "civic entrepreneurs." The term *entrepreneur* suggests the extent to which a business framework underlies our model, but it also suggests the range of skills demanded by the current environment. The civic entrepreneur is motivated foremost by a deep commitment to improving the community, but also brings the following pairs of skills to bear:

- **Analytical skill** to understand the environment, combined with the
  + humanitarian sensibility to understand deeply what the community needs.
- **Creativity** to see resources where others see gaps and doors where others see barriers, combined with the
  + design and engineering skills to develop efficient, effective programs.
- **Finance skills** to accurately analyze costs and forecast revenues, combined with the
  + imaginative leadership to integrate disparate groups, combine idiosyncratic funding streams into a coherent whole.
- **Passion** to convert the skeptical and motivate the unsure, combined with the

+ **reasonableness** to know when to let go of, or change, an idea that the data do not support.

If that list sounds overwhelming, note that (1) no one said public health business planning would be easy; and (2) actually, the planning *is* often relatively easy—compared to implementation. Entrepreneurs do planning and implementation both. And you can, too.

What Can You Expect from *Public Health Business Planning*?

Our goal in this book is practical: to teach what it means to use entrepreneurial strategies for social good, and to explain key business planning skills, such as the following:

- Assessment and strategic planning
- Program planning, implementation, and evaluation
- Financial planning and budgeting
- Market research and social marketing
- Strategies for getting funded—including how to present your plan
- Project management and business plan execution strategies

The book is divided into three broad sections. The first few chapters describe the context and format for your public health business plan. Chapter 2, Defining Public Health Entrepreneurial Business Planning, presents a definition of the public health entrepreneur and a description of entrepreneurial strategies used in public health. Integrating the thinking of James Johnson and Tom Ricketts, Management Academy faculty members from the UNC schools of Business and Public Health, respectively, we describe civic entrepreneurs: what they do and how their activities relate to business planning. Business plans for public health projects will look different in each case—tailored for a specific set of resources and a specific community—but writing any type of business plan requires a common process and a set of core skills. Chapter 2 provides a broad overview of the steps in developing a business plan in public health, and the following chapter (Chapter 3) outlines the parts of a public health business plan. In the following chapters, we go through the parts of a finished business plan in detail: the basic description of your plan (Chapter 4); analysis of the "industry" in which you plan to operate (Chapter 5); demonstrating the need for your program (Chapter 6); identifying and working with competitors and partners (Chapter 7); developing a marketing strategy (Chapter 8); designing the project operations (Chapter 9); planning for evaluation (Chapter 10); analyzing risks and creating sustainability (Chapter 11);

and financial planning (Chapter 12). Each chapter that covers a section of the business plan includes a discussion of potential challenges you might find at that step and makes suggestions for getting around those challenges, and each ends with question templates that will help you populate your business plan when you come to write it. Answering these questions will give you a bare-bones beginning for every section, and what you can't answer will give you clues as to the work you need to do. If you break the task down into small parts, it does not seem so daunting, and you can begin gathering crucial information without worrying about the project as a whole.

The final set of chapters is about implementation: what you actually *do*. Chapter 13 describes a critical early step in your planning: assessing the practicality of an idea with a feasibility plan. This chapter could have gone first: you *must* be thinking about feasibility at every step of your process, and you should write the feasibility plan before you write one word of a business plan. We're assuming you will read the book before beginning your business plan, and we put feasibility where it is because you need to know about what goes into a business plan in order to know what goes into a feasibility plan. Chapter 14 traces one business plan from idea to implementation, in the form of a case study; and Chapter 15 sends you on your way with some recent data about the implementation successes of our students.

Trust the Process

All of this makes it sound neat and simple—read the chapters in order, answer the questions at the end of the chapter, and *voila!* by the end of the book you'll have a business plan. Your finished business plan will look neat and simple, but let us warn you right now: this is a messy process. For one thing, the chapters follow the order of business plan sections, but you can't do a business plan in start-to-finish order. You can't start with the definition of plan and end with financials. To do this right you need to know a little bit of everything and run several processes at once. You might understand need in your target population, start planning your program, figure out some financial parameters, think about partners, develop the plan further, go back to the numbers, ask some more partners, think through operations and go back to financials with the new data, get some new ideas from those new partners, and tweak operations—then you're back at financials, which depends upon industry analysis, which informs the risks and operations sections, which sends you back to your definition of plan. The cycle repeats as you develop the feasibility plan into the full business plan.

If you invest the time and don't get caught up in the enormity of your project, if you're flexible and hard working and not scared of revising, you'll be successful. Trust in the process.

How Do We Know What Works—Or Doesn't?

Much of the content and many examples in this book are gleaned from the Management Academy program and the team projects that have come out of that program. The Management Academy for Public Health (www.maph.unc.edu) is a mid-career public health management training program that combines a business education with a public health focus. Run jointly by the University of North Carolina School of Public Health and the UNC Kenan-Flagler Business School, the program develops high potential public health managers and their partners who attend in teams over a nine-month span. The program combines on-campus and distance learning components. The capstone project is a business plan that each team creates to address a public health challenge in their communities, a plan that they expect to implement after they complete the program. The program is housed in the North Carolina Institute for Public Health, the practice arm of the University of North Carolina School of Public Health.[6]

The Management Academy was established in 1999. It was seeded with funding from a unique public-private partnership, comprising the Centers for Disease Control and Prevention, the Health Resources and Services Administration, the Robert Wood Johnson Foundation, and the W. K. Kellogg Foundation. These four organizations came together to fund the program for a demonstration period. After four years of grant funding, the Management Academy is now self-sustaining through tuition fees. It is actually a very good example of how a program can get seed money, benefit from innovative partnering, and create a program that people are willing to pay for—that is, a program that is sustainable.

The Management Academy is not a business plan incubator. There's a lot more to the program, whose purpose is to improve both individual and organizational effectiveness through strengthening a broad range of management abilities, including how to manage people, data, money, and partnerships. For the purposes of this book, however, we will focus solely on the business planning aspects of the program. We have learned much about public health business planning through developing and running the Management Academy for Public Health. Specifically, the experiences of our participants with their business plans have helped us see what works and what doesn't in the real world when attempting to apply business-like thinking to the public health enterprise. Throughout this book we use examples from real business plans written by real people who have completed our program.

Not all of these business plans were implemented, and sometimes we'll use them as examples of what not to do. But many of them were implemented and represent exciting new ways your colleagues from across the country are meeting the public health challenges that face us all. Here is a sampling of initiatives that started with business plans from the Management Academy for Public Health:

- A program to integrate behavioral health care into a rural public health system in Buncombe County, North Carolina, effecting state-level changes in policy and funding mechanisms for mental health service delivery.
- A residential facility for at-risk pregnant women in southeast Georgia, saving the health system millions of in-patient care dollars for low-income mothers-to-be.
- A workforce development initiative to create a certificate program for public health workers in Milwaukee, in collaboration with the University of Wisconsin-Milwaukee.
- An exercise program for kids, developed in partnership with the YMCA in Wilmington, North Carolina.
- A plan to diversify funding and expand service offerings by a non-profit HIV-AIDS clinic in Florence, South Carolina. The clinic used their business plan to earn Community Health Center designation.
- A waste water treatment plan for residents of a rural Virginia community.

Many of these examples relate to health care. That is partly because health care–related plans lend themselves to the processes we describe in this book. Business planning won't apply to everything you have to do in a public health organization: some of your responsibilities are mandated and paid for by the state, or mandated and not paid for but expected to be free, or not the type of thing that an outside partner would be interested in getting involved with. Note that all of these examples use community partners to greatly leverage the input of public health agencies.

Throughout this book, we'll use parts of these teams' business plans—and many others—to illustrate our points. You won't find a complete business plan reproduced in here for a couple of reasons. First, there are no perfect business plans. Every business plan created for the Management Academy has stronger points and weaker points. The weaker points may or may not doom the plan to failure, but in any event we want you to imitate the strong points, so that's mostly what we share. If we were to write a perfect, generic plan, just to illustrate what one would look like, you might be more discouraged than inspired. We believe it's more important to show you what others have done in the real world than set up a faultless ideal. Finally, each plan is different because each idea is different. So, while parts of other people's business plans may fit perfectly with what you want to do, chances are their whole plan will not. If you still want to see a full plan, we provide many full-text business plans on the program's website, www.maph.unc.edu.

Just once in here, however, we do trace the creation of a plan from start to finish, to give you an idea of what might be involved in writing a plan and getting it implemented. The 2005 South Carolina Management Academy team that created and implemented the HIV clinic plan mentioned above agreed to share their ongoing story with us. We share it with you in Chapter 14 in case study format, where we attempt to translate what they did into what you can do. This and many more examples will, we hope, inspire you to try our methods.

What We're *Not* Doing in This Book

We recognize the political connotations in the word *business*. We are trying to define the word broadly as a way of analyzing possibilities, planning strategies, and creating sustainable outcomes. We know that it may be construed very narrowly and may be resisted by your constituents or colleagues. Some of you might see red flags in the language of entrepreneurial public health business planning and think we're recommending a move to fully privatize the public health enterprise. We are not. We recognize the differences between the public and the private sectors in terms of risk-taking; we understand the distinctions between state-mandated activities and the choices open to businesses in a free market. We contend instead that the process of developing a business plan is a useful process in some specific cases. In our experience, many public health entities have found it beneficial to build revenue generation into particular programs with particular partners, and we have great examples of these. And, we *do* strongly recommend finding partners from outside of governmental public health to help identify and tackle new ways of addressing challenges.

So, our goal is to open your eyes to new ways of attacking problems, and we hope to set the bar high with regard to thinking beyond the confines of traditional public health parameters. We will also show how the tools we're about to describe—including entrepreneurial thinking, community needs assessment, strategic partnering, financial planning, program design and evaluation, and social marketing—can help create and sustain a phenomenal program, without abandoning the public sector.

We hope you'll learn from the work of your colleagues from across the United States and find it as remarkable—and inspiring—as we do.

References

1. Johnson, James, Jr., et al. The crucible of public health practice: major trends shaping the design of the Management Academy for Public Health. *J Public Health Management Practice*, 12(5): 419–425, 2006.

2. An example of a public health agency that has codified how programs will be assessed is DeKalb County, Georgia. Their "Methodology for Assessing and Ranking Board of Health Programs and Functions" (unpublished) lists several steps and criteria for ranking programs in the areas of services offered (is it a core function of public health? is the program effective in the achievement of its stated goals and objectives?); fiscal issues (how many dollars of revenue are produced by this program? how much money would the board of health save if the program were eliminated?); and external issues (are the services provided used by a large number of people, and would they be concerned if services were eliminated? would the curtailment/elimination of this program result in adverse political or social reaction within the community?). Being able to answer these questions accurately (and in the affirmative) is key to remaining a high priority program.

3. Washington, DC: National Academies Press.

4. Porter, Janet E., and Edward L. Baker. Partnering essentials. *Journal of Public Health Management & Practice* 11(2): 174–177, March/April 2005.

5. Collins, Jim. *Good to Great and the Social Sectors: A Monograph to Accompany Good to Great*. Boulder, CO: Jim Collins, 2005.

6. For an overview of the program, its development and outcomes, see the *Journal of Public Health Management and Practice*, 12: 5 (September/October 2006), a special issue entirely devoted to the Management Academy for Public Health. See also the website at www.maph.unc.edu.

Chapter 2

Defining Public Health Entrepreneurial Business Planning

I f the ideas we're presenting here seem daunting, remember—you're already doing business-type planning! We're trying to give you some tools for doing it more effectively, or more systematically, but the bottom line is, you are already responding to current realities by assessing needs, working with a range of partners to address those needs, hammering out budgets and finding new ways to fund your programs, and "selling" your programs to a variety of constituents. We know you can't do *everything* you need to do through business planning, but you can—and already do—do a lot that is "entrepreneurial."

The Civic Entrepreneur

The phrase "public health entrepreneurial business planning" has many connotations, some of them contradictory. It implies that you should think innovatively and imaginatively about the public health challenges you face, and also apply cold-hearted analysis to the solutions you dream up to address those challenges. You cannot be averse to risk but also cannot court risk unnecessarily. You embrace both idealistic goals and realistic budget numbers. You plan for the future, while understanding the past and keeping track of facts in the present.

In public health and the nonprofit sector, your work is to "create the conditions under which people can be healthy" in your community. Applying business-like thinking to this endeavor is "civic entrepreneurship." A civic entrepreneur is a mission- and community-driven engine for starting things up, expanding things, and keeping things going. The way a civic entrepreneur accomplishes these tasks is not that different from how their counterparts in the private sector start and sustain their enterprises.

Entrepreneurs of any stripe undertake many of the same activities on a day-to-day or project-by-project basis. These activities involve figuring out the community's needs; building teams to help address these needs; brainstorming solutions; analyzing and whittling down possible solutions; raising money for start-up; keeping track of a solution's success at fulfilling the originally diagnosed need; and, finally, figuring out how to keep it all going. Each of these activities corresponds to part of the business planning process.

Entrepreneurs Find Out What's Needed

Private entrepreneurs try to "fill a niche" or meet a demand among their potential customers. The similarity with public health is clear: health assessment is an "essential service" of public health,[1] foundational to everything we do. Health assessment involves finding out the current state of the public's health and what the public needs in order to be healthy and safe. That means collecting all kinds of data, both quantitative (demographics, employment, health care utilization) and qualitative (what specific groups perceive as health needs). It means identifying trends, gathering input and information from a broad spectrum of sources, and synthesizing these findings into knowledge that informs next steps. The best entrepreneurs know the details about "conditions on the ground": they have studied a group closely and learned what that group needs and wants. In this respect, entrepreneurs are scientific.

As a public health civic entrepreneur, you can use this scientific assessment to ascertain and demonstrate the need and target market for initiatives you plan to implement. To an audience of political leaders, potential funders, or community partners, you can use these data to show how important the problem is, who is affected, and why it is worth solving. You can prove that you've consulted with members of the target group to understand their concerns. You can compare the cost—in dollar terms, lives affected, and future conditions created—of funding your idea vs. the costs of failing to address this problem.

Different audiences will need different data. Political leaders will want to know not only fiscal impact but also intangible costs and benefits, for example, how the image of the governmental entity will be affected by this project. In a project planned and implemented by a Management Academy team from New Hanover County, North Carolina, the building of a spay-neuter facility at the Animal Control Services led not only to higher rates of pet sterilization and money saved on euthanizing unwanted pets, but also, unexpectedly, to higher customer satisfaction, higher rates of pet adoption, and a more positive image for the animal shelter.[2] Being able to predict the intangible benefits of your endeavors, as well as the more concrete returns, will help you "sell" your idea to a broad constituency.

Knowing what's needed goes a long way toward knowing what needs to be done. Several years ago, public health workers in a small county in eastern Ohio were recognized by the National Association of County and City Health Organizations (NACCHO) for their work on a project to reduce vehicle accidents between cars and horse-drawn buggies. The solution involved (1) producing educational materials to inform the Amish about how to safely co-exist with automobiles on the highways, and (2) working with Amish community members to design battery-powered lighting devices appropriate to Amish belief systems. Taking the time to collect local knowledge and make local connections was clearly essential to that project. Other cases may not be so obvious, but good needs assessment is always necessary.

Entrepreneurs Brainstorm

Entrepreneurs combine the practical, scientific base with the flexibility to imagine possibilities. The term *entrepreneur* suggests a person who welcomes audacious ideas, imagines unusual future states, plays "what if" games, brainstorms. In general, we expect entrepreneurs to have ideas: more ideas, and wackier ideas, than a regular person. The best entrepreneurs, of course, also have the judgment to recognize the ideas that have the most merit. This ability to understand how likely it is that an idea will work, and what the potential "payoff" will be if it does, is a valuable skill that can only be developed through trial and error.

Innovation is a hot topic in American business. The computer/ Internet revolution that started in the 1990s helped produce big gains in efficiency and productivity. Today, fewer big gains are to be made by improving productivity in business. Instead businesses now look for innovative ideas to produce the next big gains.

Brainstorming is not primarily a game of quality: it is first a game of quantity. The way to win is to generate the most ideas. The most diverse team will usually win because it will have a bigger universe of ideas. The entrepreneur's role in this game is to list all the possibilities, to look where a good idea might be *and* where a good idea couldn't possibly be (to paraphrase *The Wheel on the School*).

Brainstorming extends beyond the basic question of "What can our public health agency do about problem X?" Entrepreneurs brainstorm about partners, too: "Who else works on this problem in the community, and how can we work with them, or learn from them?" They challenge scale and duration assumptions: "How can we think even bigger or longer-term about this problem?" They brainstorm new funding sources: "How can we do this without costing the public more tax dollars or scrambling to get a grant again in five years?" In other words, brainstorming should include asking questions that aren't always asked in risk-averse governmental organizations.

Entrepreneurs Analyze

The necessary counterbalance to brainstorming is analysis. Create, then edit. Entrepreneurs must be wildly creative in coming up with ideas, and then they must be carefully analytical to figure out which ones have merit. They must be analytical in designing "evidence-based" ways of operationalizing their ideas, but they must be creative in seeing beyond the ways things have been done in the past in order to locate efficiencies.

Entrepreneurs often find themselves ahead of the hard evidence. Sometimes their optimism allows them to find possibilities in ideas that seem to have already failed: they can see how adjustments in design or execution might have prevented an otherwise good idea from succeeding.

The holy grail of an electronic medical record system is a good example. For years, optimists have been predicting that electronic medical records could improve health for huge groups by letting key information about patients and their medical histories be shared systematically by different parts of the health care system. Such systems could potentially improve communication between practitioners, continuity of care across sites, information and reference data at each site, and organizational quality outcomes. Public health would improve as individual and community health status improved. Unfortunately, virtually anyone who worked to help health data systems talk to each other had a horror story about the results. The difference in these stories from project to project and from state to state was generally in the number of years and amount of money that ultimately got wasted.

These setbacks haven't stopped the work, as inexorably the technology, the policy, and the culture have shifted. In 2006, a Management Academy team from South Carolina took advantage of these shifts and partnered with a regional hospital and a nonprofit providers' group to create a plan to develop an electronic medical record (EMR) system in the rural Lakelands area of their state. Their plan, which is now being successfully implemented, was to share the cost of a sustainable EMR between the rural hospital and regional providers. Public health has a strong interest in the project because, in addition to assuring better care for individuals, it holds the promise of providing much better aggregate health data about a widely spread rural population.

The point of brainstorming and analysis is to come up with a workable new idea for addressing the identified need. Now, the group that was looking at your data is hearing your idea. They want the story. What is the problem, what is the solution, whose lives are affected? What resources will you put toward this problem, and where will you get them? What other stories can be compared to yours? Who else has attempted to solve this problem, and how? They do not want to hear a story they've heard before: they want a fresh solution, tailored to the situation that exists here, today.

Entrepreneurs Build Teams

In the American mythology, entrepreneurs work alone: we picture a "great man" having a eureka moment, waiting for something to blow up, hit him on the head, electrocute his kite. Partners do fit in this myth if they are twins: see Orville and Wilbur. That "great man" story is a myth. We now know it overlooks great women, for instance. It also overstates the importance of the individual as opposed to the team.

Many of the "great woman" stories we tell involve mobilizing networks: the Suffragettes, for instance, or in public health, Margaret Sanger.[3] So the "great person" story is counterbalanced by the "great team" story. Steven Jobs didn't build and design all those Apple computers and iPods by himself: he helped mobilize people who could move an idea to a plan and a plan to a product.

Apple's history provides a case study for the importance of networking. The company's recent resurgence, exemplified by the dominant market position of the iPod, is built on a shift toward well-conceived alliances. First Apple made important alliances within the computer industry, with IBM and now Intel, to make their hardware platforms more structurally similar to PCs. Then they made key alliances *outside* the computer industry with music, audio, and video content providers: people who sell songs, shows, movies, podcasts and other content on the iTunes website.

The ability to create alliances is essential in public health for some of the same reasons. Organizations don't stand alone in the 21st century; they have to find their place in a global network of organizations.

Economies are like food chains, describing a network of complex connections between organizations, and exponential change in travel and communication networks keeps increasing the reach of that network. The best entrepreneurs know how to work the network.

If you are in governmental public health, especially at the local level, success similarly depends on your ability to be a broker-connector-convener within a network of organizations and communities. Public health is too broad and too complex for a single organization to get outcomes on its own. By definition, the best public health programs work not only at the individual level but also at the organizational or community level, by creating changes that have an impact on conditions for large groups. Ergo, coordination is critical.

So, a common strategy for creating more health is to work across organizations. That strategy has important implications for you as an entrepreneur within an organization. For instance: entrepreneurial public health organizations might do well to maximize the range of backgrounds represented on the staff, to increase the ability of the whole team to connect with as many different kinds of organizations as possible. Communication and networking skills might be key personnel selection factors: interorganizational projects succeed or fail in part based on the ability of managers and leaders to cross organizational boundaries. This means that what is commonly seen as a weakness about the public health workforce—that too few workers have degrees from schools of public health—may in fact be a strength to be leveraged. We won't go too far with that—some of our best friends have degrees from schools of public health, and the discipline-specific knowledge that informs public health educators, nurses, epidemiologists, biostatisticians, and environmental scientists, to name a few, is knowledge that adds value to public health organizations. But we would make the point that organizations should recognize value in staff members who can communicate effectively (write, speak, and listen) across disciplinary boundaries.

We have countless examples of the value of cross-disciplinary planning from the Management Academy. In the spay-neuter project mentioned earlier in the chapter, the team included a veterinarian from a local animal hospital. Besides being instrumental in helping design the surgery space, this individual provided a connection with the veterinarian community, which initially saw the spay-neuter clinic as a threat to their business but came to see it as an ally in their quest to reduce the population of unwanted pets and bring more pet owners into the animal health care system. The team that created the residential facility for at-risk pregnant women in Georgia included a local perinatologist on their team. Depending on the project, teams can include medical professionals, businesspeople in related fields, and professionals from local nonprofits working on similar issues. Projects that address public safety may include first responders; those that address school health usually include senior personnel and/or nursing staff from the local schools. Others include academics working on relevant topics in their research or practice activities. Such partners add value to the project through their varied expertise or experiences, their connection with others in the community, and the different vantage points from which they see the problem and its solution. If you can bring them on board and communicate effectively across the disciplinary divide, your projects are more successful for it.

Entrepreneurs Are Hardworking and Flexible

In our experience training state and local teams, we have found many of the best teams to resemble each other in important ways: they spend lots of time together, they share the work, they feed off the energy of teammates, they seek out experts and make benchmarking trips, they get consumed by their projects, and they spend much more time and energy than they planned. Many of them wind up at the end with very different projects from the ones they started with. This suggests flexibility in the team, but also suggests that whether or not you start out with a good idea doesn't seem to be a critical success factor. More important is how hard you work to generate new ideas as you go, and how well you are able to rank and prioritize and carry out those ideas as a team.

Entrepreneurs Find the Money

Entrepreneurs are ambitious: they want to make something happen. Money fuels that reaction. Some entrepreneurs are ambitious for themselves; they want to make the big score, turn a clever idea and a lot of hard work into cash with which to buy a basketball team, say, as Mark Cuban did. But as David Gergen notes about the three presidents for whom he worked in the late 20th century, successful leaders (political and otherwise) are ambitious for others.[4] David Bornstein's book *How to Change the World* tells the stories of several social entrepreneurs whose ambitions are directed primarily to serving others.[5]

No matter the goal, entrepreneurs need resources to fuel the change they want to make. They go to their friends and families and present to venture capital groups, trying to get the cash they need to get started. In public health the situation is quite similar, except that we tend to go to politicians, government agencies, or foundations for cash.

The key difference between the private entrepreneur and the social entrepreneur is the order in which these steps occur. Governmental and nonprofit public health organizations often do these steps backward:

first we look for granting organizations that are offering money, then we come up with a plan, within their budget, to get that money. Forward-thinking public health organizations have learned to be more intentional. First they decide what they want to do; they determine what resources they will need to do it; then they initiate contact with funders or negotiate to adjust the requirements on grants to better fit local needs and objectives.

An example of a forward-thinking organization is the Buncombe County, North Carolina, Health Center (BCHC). Responding to a growing need for mental health care in their community, the BCHC sought funding from various stakeholders, and, through their support, instituted a fully integrated behavioral health program in 2004. The BCHC has now joined forces with other partners in the state to address state-wide policy changes in how the state funds such programs. The resulting changes will improve behavioral health care for the poor across the state.[6]

Success at launching a great new product or service is fundamentally dependent on the entrepreneur's ability to find resources to get the project started: hiring people, for instance, or buying materials to create something valuable for "customers." The long-term success of many projects is dependent on whether or not the project continues to generate those resources. So "Find the Money" is less a one-time egg hunt than it is a search for a roosting hen: you need to find (or create) continuing sources to sustain life.

Entrepreneurs Start It Up

Entrepreneurs take risks. The best entrepreneurs know how to minimize risks; they eliminate needless risks; they study past failures to understand and avoid risks. But their aversion to *unnecessary* risk does not prevent them from starting up new businesses even when the outcomes aren't guaranteed. Stephen Covey says that failure provides evidence of trying hard.[7] Herman Melville claims that failure is a requirement for success: "Failure is the true test of greatness. And if it be said, that continual success is a proof that a man wisely knows his powers—it is only to be added, that, in that case, he knows them to be small."[8] In other words, if you always succeed, you haven't done much. Entrepreneurs do not want to stay carefully within their own small powers; they want to make big and meaningful change.

Public health leaders often are averse to risk, and their organizational cultures do not tolerate risk very well. This is probably due to the politics involved and the perceptions of governmental or organizational pressures to succeed. But no matter the reason, most of us do not appreciate the learning opportunities in failure. The reasons are many: human nature, the inclination of scientists to want plenty of (positive) evidence before launching an intervention, the pressures of being responsible for government money, the political and logistical hurdles inherent in government organizations. As an entrepreneur in public health, you will be working against those strains.

Barriers are to be expected: plan for them. Good plans help the implementers avoid barriers, or give them tools for getting around and through barriers. Indeed, that's one of the central criteria for defining a good business plan: will the plan work? Is it implementable? Does it deal with the obvious barriers? Your skills in scientific inquiry and innovative brainstorming will help you answer these questions. Inquire into past successes and failures, and brainstorm all the possible things that could go wrong and how you will respond when they do. Successful entrepreneurs are able to convince decision makers to implement despite the risks. Your business plan can help show that the risks are known, have been carefully analyzed, and can be managed. They also show that the potential pay-off in health is worth the risk.

Entrepreneurs Keep It Going

In the business world, "sustainability" is the hot topic. UNC's Kenan-Flagler Business School offers a concentration in "sustainable enterprise" to MBA students who want to apply their business skills to international development or urban renewal projects. The popular "Gen-X" style business magazine *Fast Company* has an annual feature on the best sustainable nonprofits, called the "Social Capitalist Awards." These entrepreneurs want to create social capital: they want to create wealth (or health, or education) for communities, via a system that will not deplete the community's resources.

In the world of local public health, where most services are ultimately delivered, *sustainability* is now a household word as well. Lots of public health work is underwritten by foundations or by federal and state agencies in the form of grants; granting organizations increasingly ask for sustainability plans of their current and prospective grantees. If you have worked very long in public health, you know why: because so many grant-funded programs ultimately fail.

By requiring "sustainability plans," granting organizations force grantees to think more like entrepreneurs, to consider grant funding as start-up money to launch a fledgling program, rather than a long-term commitment to subsidize a service. Granting organizations want to be more like venture capitalists: they want to find good projects in their areas of interest and help them fly instead of falling. You may have noticed that many grants now come with technical assistance or training—the granter's way of improving their return on investment in the long term.

When we teach about sustainability, it is commonplace for someone in the room to know an example of a big, rich, grant-funded program that failed because of its scale. Such failure is due to what's called "the scaling fallacy."

Here's how this typically happens. You respond to an RFP. Say it is for $3 million to address diabetes over three years. So you design a program that costs $1 million per year to run. You hire new staff, rent them space, buy computers—easy to do when you have several million dollars in the bank. You want to start getting results for the funders as soon as you can. You can't say it out loud, but you are secretly hoping that the program will be so great that the foundation will keep funding it indefinitely.

You can't say it out loud because it's crazy! Of course the foundation can't fund it indefinitely. For one thing, the foundation staff would have nothing to do but watch you spend the money. Instead, they are busy writing more RFPs. They assume that you are building a sustainable model to do diabetes prevention—they even asked you for a sustainability plan. When they say "sustainable model," they don't mean "a model so great that we will want to keep funding it." They mean "a model so great that *other people* will want to fund it." At the end of the three years, you have a huge staff, a complex website to manage, a big lease—$1 million in annual costs—but no revenue.

The Management Academy for Public Health fell victim to this fallacy in 1999. After pulling out overhead and evaluation, our start-up grant was roughly $2.4 million to train 600 people over three years. So, naturally, we designed a program that cost roughly $4,000 per person:

$$600 \text{ people} \times \$4000 = \$2,400,000$$

Did we think that a four thousand dollar program was sustainable without continuing grant support? Well, some of us didn't think a four *hundred* dollar per person program was sustainable. And yet the funders had asked us to submit a sustainability plan. In the original grant, this section took the form of a brief exploration of how we might introduce co-pays, and our skepticism about whether local health departments or individuals would be able to support the costs. When we had to submit a more detailed sustainability plan, we wrote it as if the funders had asked us to apply for more funding. This plan got submitted early in 2001, so we had time to process the news when the funders told us, in a word, "No." In the end we did transition to a receipt-supported model, with the help of continued grant support from CDC. And we were lucky: public health agencies were flush with preparedness money when we finally transitioned to our receipt-supported model in 2003.

The business planning discipline encourages you to build programs that are important, efficient with resources, get good outcomes, and create their own revenue. These are the programs that avoid the scrapheap when money gets tight.

Entrepreneurs Keep Tabs

Entrepreneurs do not just start something up and then turn away to start a new business. They first set up a system of people and resources to keep track of what they've launched and make sure it is doing what it was meant to do. (Then they often *do* turn away—more about that later.) In the first stages of your planning, you described the health goals you hoped to achieve. At the same time, you have to set up a system for evaluating your progress toward those goals. This is another way being an entrepreneur overlaps with being a scientist: figure out concrete measures that will track your process and outcomes, and then use them.

Businesses do this by tracking sales, measuring customer satisfaction, or seeing how often a product comes back with a complaint, for example. Public health entrepreneurs do this by measuring patient compliance, tracking provider satisfaction, counting number of clients served: any number of measures could work, depending on what you hope to accomplish. What you measure can be a powerful incentive to managers, and the failure to measure can be a powerful statement too, to internal and external people. Eventually, for most programs, someone will ask "how do we know if this is working?" Your ability to answer that question is a key factor in determining sustainability.

Are more children aware of healthy diets after your targeted health education program? Do more drivers wear seatbelts after learning about a new state law that allows highway patrol personnel to ticket them if they don't? Does the incidence of flu infection decline after a program to inoculate children at school? How will you know unless you evaluate by asking questions, gathering statistics, measuring results? Such measurement adds value to the program. The local hospital, for example, may be willing to sponsor a health department clinic if they see proof that uninsured patients are going there instead of the emergency room when they have nonurgent care needs. Local schools love programs that can be shown to make their students healthier. Happy partners are supportive partners.

This is not to say that you have to keep running every program you start. Entrepreneurs like to start up sustainable programs, but sustainability may be best accomplished by transitioning control of a program out of your organization into a partner's control. Good entrepreneurs foresee such transitions and plan for them.

Your evaluation may also tell you that your program is not working. Notwithstanding our admonition to "keep it going," civic entrepreneurs need to know when it isn't working and know when to cut their losses. Have an exit plan for ending a program that isn't working. Entrepreneurs aren't afraid of failing. In fact, they expect failure and consider it at best a learning experience and at worst a cost of achieving success.

Entrepreneurs Get It Down on Paper

If these ideas and intentions are only floating around in your head, or even if they are stated in long-range goals or strategic planning documents, they will not become reality. The kind of planning required today in public health is converging with the kind of planning required in the business world, and that needs a business plan. The sections of this chapter track what you will have to do to create the parts of a business plan: the narrative description, the demonstration of need and target market, the definition of the plan, measurement or evaluation plans, the industry analysis and identification of competitors or partners, the budget, and the analysis of risk and exit plan. Write it all down and you have a document designed to make your case and guide your activities through a successful implementation.

References

1.   See the CDC National Public Health Performance Standards Program (NPHPS) website at http://www.cdc.gov/od/ocphp/nphpsp/.

2.   McNeil, Jean, and Elisabeth Constandy. Addressing the problem of pet over-population: the experience of New Hanover County Animal Control Services. *J Public Health Management Practice* 12: 5 (Sept/Oct, 2006): 452–455.

3.   Heifetz, Ronald A. *Leadership Without Easy Answers*. Cambridge, MA: The Belknap Press of Harvard, 1994.

4.   Gergen, David. *Eyewitness to Power: The Essence of Leadership Nixon to Clinton*. New York: Touchstone, 2000.

5.   Bornstein, David. *How to Change the World: Social Entrepreneurs and the Power of New Ideas*. Oxford/New York: Oxford UP, 2004.

6.   Mims, Susan. A sustainable behavioral health program integrated with public health primary care. *Journal Public Health Management Practice* 12: 5 (Sept/Oct 2006): 456–461.

7.   Covey, Stephen. *The Seven Habits of Highly Effective People*. New York: Simon & Schuster, 1989.

8.   Melville, Herman. "Hawthorne and His Mosses." *The Literary World*. August 17 and 24, 1850.

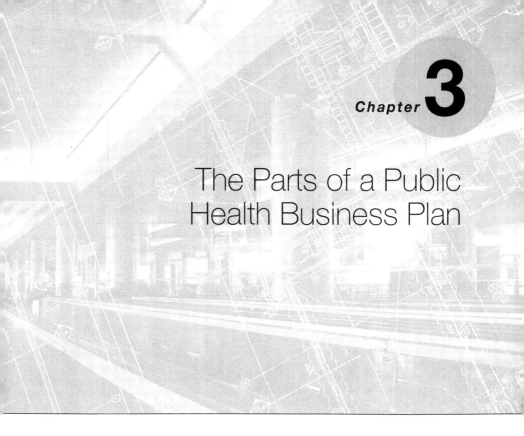

Chapter 3

The Parts of a Public Health Business Plan

A business plan should be a blueprint for how your program will be implemented. Therefore, you should describe all aspects of the program in your written plan. In this chapter we will go through all of the sections that should be included in your written business plan. This chapter is just an outline; the chapters that follow will help you develop content for the sections described here.

Business Plan Outline

The following is the outline we give to Management Academy students when they're beginning to work on their business plan:

- Executive Summary (ONE Page)
- Definition of Project
  - Product/service description
  - Customer/geographic focus
  - Objectives and measures of performance

- Industry Analysis
  - Industry structure
  - Trends
  - Threats
  - Key success factors
- Target Market Definition/Research
  - Demographics
  - Risk groups
  - Needs assessment
  - Trends
- The Competition
  - Competitors/partners
  - Barriers to entry
  - Future competition
- Marketing Strategy
  - Message
  - Media
  - Market penetration assumptions
- Operations and Management
  - Daily operations
  - Partner roles and logistics
  - Outcome measurement
  - Quality improvement
  - Information systems
  - Human resources
  - Department/agency culture
- Implementation Plan and Timeline
- Risks and Exit Plan
  - Potential risks
  - Regulations
  - Long-term development plan
  - Exit plan
- Financial Statement/Projections 3 years out
  - Narrative of budget assumptions
  - First year budget by month
  - Detailed revenue/expense budget 5 years out
  - Breakeven Analysis (optional)

This chapter will lay out the key goals for each of these sections in order to give you an overview of the whole business plan. The coming chapters will go into the details of each section, giving you rationale and context, public-health-specific guidance, real-world examples, and potential pitfalls.

We should note here that we are offering this book as a guide: these aren't requirements, but suggestions. The notion of a public health business plan is new to many organizations, so there are few expectations. Although we recommend the order and content we present here (and require them if you're a student of the Management Academy), in the real world the order and content of the sections are ultimately less important than the overall goals of the document: to analyze a business opportunity and argue for its implementation. Also, as we said before, this is the order of a finished plan, not the order in which you should create the plan: you'll go back and forth between sections at every step of the way. Finally, every plan is different because programs are different, contexts are different, communities are different, organizations and individual decision makers are different.

At the same time, you may take great comfort in knowing that, in the business world, a well-established and detailed template exists for analyzing and implementing business ideas—and that we have spent the last eight years tweaking it for public health entrepreneurs.

Executive Summary

The executive summary is the "elevator speech" of the document: the tight, punchy story of your idea in a form short enough to deliver effectively to people on their way somewhere else, with a lot on their agenda. The executive summary should describe your plan clearly and succinctly, in one page or less. "One page" in this context is an aesthetic goal, not an arbitrary rule that you should test. In other words, you want to produce one sheet of paper that looks really good: it is inviting, easy to read and easy to understand. Your one page should have plenty of white space and maybe even headings that highlight the main points.

As you would guess from its name, this one page should be a summary of everything important that's included in your plan. It isn't the introduction: it is more like the abstract of a journal article, including all the key parts in much shorter form. As such, it should not include any information not detailed elsewhere in your plan, and should not include anything that doesn't help the decision maker decide. At the very least the summary should include the highlights of your key sections: the need for the program, a description of the program itself and the target market, and the financial sustainability model. You can assume that some people will ONLY read this page; they need to understand the key points without reading any further. Although this is always the first part of the written plan, it should probably be the last section you write.

Definition of Plan

This section introduces your plan for addressing a public health problem, making a compelling argument that you have a solution to the problem. It prepares a reader/decision maker to hear and understand the detailed analysis that follows, describing the **product or service** you plan to offer: what, exactly, you are going to do, and identifying the **customer geographic focus**: who will benefit from this program and in what way. At the end of this section, the reader should understand what you are planning, without necessarily understanding all the reasons why or the analytical steps you followed in choosing this plan. This section will also outline the **objectives** that you hope to achieve through this program (not too many; few enough that readers can remember them) and the **measures** by which you can gauge whether you've reached these objectives. It is appropriate to briefly discuss the financial model here, at least enough to answer the basic questions of how revenue will be generated. We talk about how you'll actually generate the information for this section in later chapters, and Chapter 4 goes into more detail about constructing the Definition of Plan.

Industry Analysis

The goal of this section of the business plan is to understand the history of programs such as yours. A thorough analysis of the industry in which your program will operate will give you a good idea of some of the challenges faced by other organizations doing similar work, as well as some of their best practices. **Define the industry** in which you will operate in whatever way is most useful. Keep in mind that the industry is specific to your particular program; it may be most useful to think beyond public health. For example, if your program focuses on healthy eating and weight control, your industry analysis should probably look at the weight management and nutrition industry. Even if it is being implemented by a public health department, your program would be competing with other weight management products and services, and subject to the same market forces.

Your industry analysis should look at the industry as a whole, and not specifically within your geographic area. Discuss the **structure of the industry**—is it made up of a lot of small organizations, or is it dominated by a few key players? Do organizations tend to stay successful in the industry over the long term, or do many come and go often? Identify **major trends** in the industry, such as a transition to using new technologies or an additional product or service that is commonly offered. Look at **key success factors** in the industry (what factors must be in place for a program to be successful?) as well as barriers to entry (what hurdles need to be overcome in order for you to begin operating within this industry?). This section includes material that you might know as benchmarking and "evidence-based practice" research:

again, the goal is to understand the history of programs such as yours in order to use best practices and avoid well-known pitfalls.

Developing this content is described more fully in Chapter 5.

Demonstration of Need and Target Market

In this section, describe how you know the need exists for your program, and convince your audience that the problem is worth solving. Be clear about the nature of the gap that your program is intended to fill. You will also discuss the customer and geographic focus of your program. Define your specific market (i.e., by zip code or county) and include demographic information regarding the size and needs of this market. Maps and other visual aids can be very helpful here and are recommended. Identify what segment of the market you are targeting (i.e., elderly within that zip code). Show what need is not being met efficiently and why clients are not benefiting from current services. Show pertinent data (quantitative and qualitative) to demonstrate need in the specific geographic area targeted. Compare the benefits of funding this program to the costs inherent in failing to fund it. Be sure to look at both tangible and intangible benefits. Identify specific risk groups that your program will aid. You will also want to describe the physical environment in which your program will operate: what is the geographic area in your community? How many people live there? What other information about the area is pertinent to your program?

Developing content for this section is described in Chapter 6.

Competitors/Partners

This section has two key functions in public health: describing competitors, and then describing partners (some of the competitors will probably appear on the partners list).

The first function is to describe the competitive landscape: what other organizations offer products or services similar to those that your program will offer? Include indirect competition—other organizations that offer other services that meet the need that you are planning to meet, even if the service isn't exactly the same. Because markets change over time, you should identify what potential **future competition** you anticipate. There will be some form of competition for any program— the key is identifying the competition in order to define your program's competitive advantage. A common mistake is to describe why a program is so unique that there is no competition; keep looking.

Part of the competition analysis is to think about **barriers to entry**. In other words, what things make it difficult to start something new in this area? If the barriers are difficult because you need lots of money to get started, or because people rely on trusted brands in this industry, you will need to show that you can clear the barriers. If the barriers are low, it means anybody can jump into the market, so others might be following you in the future and taking away your customers.

Some of your competitors may work as **partners**. Who are possible community/state/national partners? How will this program fit in with their goals and objectives? What will they contribute to the program? Is the local environment receptive to this sort of plan?

For each of the organizations you list in this section, be it competitor or partner, you should include a description of the organization and its product or service offering. Ultimately you want to be able to show that your product or service is distinctive relative to competitors in the marketplace.

Chapter 7 describes identifying and working with partners and competitors in more detail.

Marketing Strategy

A marketing strategy outlines how you will get your message out to potential clients. Your marketing strategy will have three main components. The first component is your **message.** What information do you want to convey to potential clients? Will you have a slogan for your program? Will you design a logo to represent it? What are the three key points you want to get across?

The second component is your choice of how you will spread your message to others. **Media** can include something as basic as in-house brochures or inter-office memos, or something as involved as television or radio commercials. Do not assume your intended customers will automatically understand the value of your program and flock to use it. All programs will need some form of marketing to reach their audience, and you will need to include funds for marketing in your budget.

The third component of your marketing strategy is your **market penetration** assumptions. That is, exactly how many people can you expect to reach (how far into the market can you penetrate) with each marketing medium? Here you will have to do some research and/or make some assumptions. For example, if you are planning to air a commercial (or Public Service Announcement) on the radio, what is the listening audience of the radio station during the time of day that your commercial (or PSA) will be aired? If you are planning to send out a mailing, how many people are on your mailing list? Market penetration assumptions should be specific and quantitative.

Chapter 8 covers developing a marketing strategy.

Project Operations and Management

In this section, describe the nuts and bolts of how your program will be run. First you must consider what **resources** you will require to run the program, including human resources, technology and/or information systems, and facilities or space you will require.

This is the place to describe the **daily operations** of the program, the activities to be performed and responsible parties, the experience of a client going through the program or receiving your services, and the role your partners may play in day-to-day operations.

Define **measures of success** for your program here, in detail (these will line up with the measures you presented in the first section). What outcome measures will you use to determine whether your program is filling the needs it is intended to address? Outcome measures must be specific and quantifiable, and each outcome measure must have a specific time period associated with it so that at the end of that time period you will know how you are progressing compared with your goals for where you wanted to be at that point. Alongside outcome measures, describe the **quality improvement** methods you will use if you cannot meet your goals. Chapter 9 describes this project operations and management content in more detail. We discuss measures and evaluation planning in Chapter 10.

Implementation Plan and Timeline

In this section, share the plan for implementing your program, including a timeline with specific dates by which you expect to implement key actions or reach certain milestones. This plan should include milestones for getting the program up and running as well as for the operational phase of the plan. As with the outcome measures, these milestones should be specific enough that it will be clear whether you have met your goals based on the timeline you lay out. Detail is helpful, because it will improve your planning and your outcomes. You might want to do a timeline graphic that shows critical events, tasks that overlap, and who takes the lead on different tasks. Look for more detail in Chapter 9.

Risks and Exit Plan

Risk is inherent in any new venture. You should analyze **potential risks** before implementing your program and develop a plan to overcome any possible barriers. Think about risks at all levels—legal, political, regulatory, technological, economic, and financial. Once you have identified potential risks, define your plan to overcome these risks. A strong plan will outline any and all potential risks, rather than glossing over the importance of risk.

You also need to develop an **exit strategy**. First you must determine whether the program will be run by the public health department for the long term, whether another organization would take over operations, or whether the program will be spun off into its own entity. Describe how this will be accomplished. Also, you will need to determine at what point the decision will be made that the program is not successful and needs to be shut down, detailing how that will occur. If you have assets, will they be sold off or merged with the health department's resources? How will your clients be taken care of? Attention to these details shows that you have planned for the most likely risks; it also shows that, in addition to thinking about how to bring the plan in to the organization, you have also thought about how to transition the plan out if necessary.

Exit planning in public health is critically important because in many cases, the governmental public health entities are most interested in the planning and implementation of a plan like this: you may be less interested in continuing to do the work forever. For public health business planning, the exit plan section encourages you to plan for some partners to take over operations at some future stage.

Chapter 11 considers risks and exit planning, and how they relate to long-term sustainability.

Financials

The goal of this section is to demonstrate that your idea is efficient and has a reasonable chance of sustaining itself financially. In the private sector, financial success is in itself an outcome: in the public sector, financial sustainability is a means to an end (more healthy communities). You want to show that the program will create value: health per dollar.

To reach that goal, you will want to describe the financial needs for running your program in detail, showing all the **costs** to start it up and keep it running over the long term. You must also describe how you will pay for those expenses: in addition to estimating the **revenue** you will generate, you might include resources such as gifts or grant monies to be used for start-up and partner in-kind donations. This section contains a **budget narrative** that spells out your budget **assumptions**, a **first year budget by month**, a detailed **revenue/ expense budget five years out**, and an optional **breakeven analysis**, depending on how your plan generates revenue, to highlight your assumptions about expected volume and revenue.

Financial planning is discussed more fully in Chapter 12.

Briefly, On Style

This book is not a writing guide, but we have three guidelines that should dictate how you put this all together.

1. Use Plain Language

You may have learned in school that more words + bigger words = a better grade from your teacher. You may have learned that more complexity means you're smarter. Both may be true in high school or college. Neither is true in the real world. Your goal in most of your writing at work is to get somebody to do something. This business plan is no different: you are trying to get decision makers/funders to say "yes, great idea, go ahead, how much should we make the check out for?" They can't do that if they don't understand you. They won't do that if they get the impression you aren't a very clear thinker (as evidenced by unclear writing). Also, in some settings these plans may be public documents, and readability will be critical to your constituents' perceptions of how you are doing your job.

Using plain language first means using common words: you do not want your reader to struggle to understand. Plain language also means direct sentences: "Examination of bids by interested persons shall be permitted…" is bureaucratic. "You may examine bids" is direct. It also puts the reader in the foreground with the "you."

Think also about "empty" or weak verbs. "The system **has** wide applicability for a variety of industrial situations" is weak. "The system **applies** to a variety of industrial situations" is stronger. Finally, look for "camouflaged verbs," words that end in -ion, -tion, -ment, -ant, -ent, -ence, -ance, -ency, and replace them with active verbs. For example, "A suspen**sion** of these programs by the director will occur until his reevalua**tion** of their progress is complete" can become "The director will **suspend** these programs until he **reevaluates** their progress."

If you want to make your writing clearer and stronger, get yourself a good writers' handbook and read it. Or attend the Management Academy. We have a good writing clinic session.

2. Design Your Document for the Greatest Readability

Whether they realize it or not, your readers will form an impression of your plan the minute they look at your document or data display, before they've read or heard one word. So, you might want to think about the appearance.

Choose your typeface for greatest readability. Usually, serif types (Times New Roman) are good for blocks of text on the page. Not so great for slides. Sans serif types (Arial) are great for headings and PowerPoint slides, but reading paragraph after paragraph in sans serif is hard on the eyes. One of the best business plans we've ever received—in terms of planning detail and sustainability—is one of the worst we ever received in terms of what it looked like. With small typeface and small margins, the team fit a lot of information in, at the expense of the reader's eyesight! We use it every year as an example of what not to do when it comes to formatting. Your typeface should ideally be 12 pt, your margins at least one inch on all sides.

Use enough white space—margins, indentations, spaces between paragraphs—to avoid daunting your reader with giant blocks of words. Headings are a good way to break up text. It is important that headings say something useful. "Cost of Diabetes Treatment in Hale County" is better than "Background," for instance. By posing a question that is answered in the text—"Why Provide Case Management?"—headings can similarly prepare readers for what follows.

Use bold and other formatting styles strategically. Too much, and your reader won't look at anything closely. Too little, and you've got a long, traditional paragraph that may lose the attention of your audience. A traditional paragraph about a recommendation is not as effective, sometimes, as a schematic paragraph with a bold recommendation followed by bullet points explaining your reasoning. Key words in each bullet could also be set in bold.

The organization of your ideas also affects readability. If you build up to your point, make the build-up clear and not too long. "First this, then this, and therefore, we recommend this." It often works to start with your bottom line and then explain—"Our target market will be teenagers" (and then say why); "Two entities will be competing for this market" (and then explain who they are). Remember, some readers will only skim your document—you want them to get your idea even if they only read the headings or first sentences of paragraphs.

If you really want to improve your readability, have your friends and colleagues who don't know anything about your project read your plan. Then, listen to what they ask you. Are they asking you questions that you thought you answered in your plan? If so, go back and revise: it's your problem if your audience doesn't understand you.

3. Paint the Picture

Use multiple means to get your point across. Words are good, but paragraph after paragraph of standard prose will bore your reader, and their interest (and support) will flag, no matter how skillfully you write and format your document. Present pictures, maps, quotations, graphs, tables—anything to illustrate your point for them, so they can see what you envision. Think about how you might need a graph to understand a difficult scientific point, or how much meaning is added to a news story when it includes interviews with eye witnesses.

But we're getting ahead of ourselves. Don't get caught up in style now, before you've even written a word. Read the rest of this book, write your plan, and then come back and think about revision and editing.

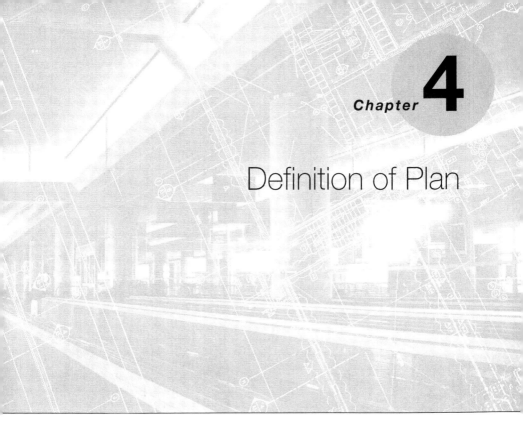

Chapter 4

Definition of Plan

Don't judge a book by its cover: often good advice. There is no prohibition against judging a book by its first chapter, though, and history suggests that your business plan will certainly be judged by its first section.

The definition of plan section of your business plan is your chance to make a first impression. First and most important, this first section introduces your idea. It prepares a reader to understand the detailed analysis that follows. The second function is to summarize—perhaps "simplify" or "clarify" are better terms—the plan you have come up with. At the end of this section, the reader should understand exactly what you are planning to do. Later you will outline the analytical steps you followed. For now, the goal is to "paint the picture" so your reader knows what you are proposing and why. You want to describe the project very early and as clearly as you can so that your audience will understand the later detail sections.

Clarity and Specificity

Your first job is to be clear and specific. Avoid jargon at all costs. Every year at the Management Academy we have teams that present their plans—they hand out a glossy, bound document, show their PowerPoint slides, talk through their practiced speeches—but after ten minutes, no one in the room understands what, exactly, they want to do.

If you say you're going to "be the interface between community, work, and family" or "help organizations through unique products and innovative training" (we made these up, but they sound familiar, don't they?), your audience may be intrigued, but they will also be confused. Throw away your mission statements and boilerplates: they're full of language like this, language that sounds good but doesn't inform. Start over with a clear description of exactly what you are going to do. Will you provide prescription drugs to uninsured children in your community? Say that. Will you partner with a local employer to provide preventive health screenings such as mammography and colonoscopies to employees? Say that. Will you work with community leaders to run an after-school athletics program for teens? Train local hospital staff in emergency preparedness? Educate food preparers about food safety at local restaurants? Educate teachers to look for signs of dating abuse among teens? All of these are specific, clear statements. Make sure your definition of plan is made up of this type of statement.

Some readers appreciate a comparison with a model to make an idea more specific or concrete. What existing programs or parts of programs did you model your idea on? This is the stereotypical way that movie ideas get pitched in Hollywood. "It's a romantic comedy set in New Orleans after the hurricane—*You've Got Mail* meets *Twister*." Your idea might be a combination of familiar parts too: a mobile van for pet services; an emergency planning program for childcare centers; an electronic medical record for rural primary care providers; a fitness program for a network of churches. Telling your reader about other programs that did something like what you want to do will help them understand your program better.

What Goes into the Definition of Plan?

Include as part of your overview some information about the scope of the plan, how the plan is to be financed, who it serves, where, and what you expect to achieve.

Scope

A good, convincing plan has a reasonable scope. If you take the time to put your plan into specific terms, you will be able to test its reasonableness. Be sure you know the difference here between aspirations and expectations. You may aspire to save the world from diabetes. If you write that in the definition of plan, your reader will say that's not reasonable: what do you *expect*? You may expect to lower the incidence of diabetes by helping people develop healthy lifestyle choices. Develop a plan to encourage healthy living, defined as improving diet and increasing exercise, among a specific group of people—African American women, for example. Write that in your definition of plan, and people will know what you aspire to *and* what you expect.

Finance

It is appropriate to briefly discuss the financial model in this section. Two financially related questions are paramount for decision makers. First, they are interested in start-up funds and long-term sustainable revenues. How will the program get started and keep going? Second, they are interested in cost and benefit. In other words, will the plan be effective (will it work) and efficient (will it work for cheap)? Don't share your full analysis here; just prepare the reader for what is coming in the finance chapter.

Market and Geographic Focus

Later in the plan you will present a chapter on the target market, but it is also appropriate to lay the groundwork for that chapter here. Describe who will benefit from this program, and in what way. You may have a geographical focus; describe it in enough depth so your reader is prepared.

Objectives and Measures

Outline the objectives that you hope to achieve through this program (not too many; few enough so that readers can remember them). Choose logical, achievable objectives that can be measured, and share a few key measures (no more than two or three). Fundamentally, you want to tell us what success would look like. What would be a "home run" for this program?

Organizing the Definition of Plan Section

The definition of plan should make a clean start, as if the executive summary did not exist. Indeed, some readers will skip the executive summary and start with this section. Don't refer to things or use acronyms that you introduced in the executive summary. You might start writing this section first—you might work on this section last. You should probably do both. This section draws on information that you present in greater depth later on, so make sure you re-edit this section carefully when you finish with the rest of the business plan. In fact, in the messy world of public health business planning, you're sure to go back to this section several times as you gather data and write the other sections of your plan.

The logic of your plan should drive what you say and how you organize this section. Beyond that, we do have a couple of suggestions for drafting and revising this section:

1. In drafting the definition of plan, imagine you are explaining the plan to a friend or a colleague. You want to find a good narrative flow—almost a story. And you want to use simple, plain language: use the words and simple structures you would use in talking.
2. Make sure that, at the end of this section, readers understand what you plan to do and how you plan to do it.
3. Ideally there will be no big surprises for the reader after this section. Most of the rest of the plan will be the justification or the logistical specifics of what you've presented here. This section should provide a map of the rest of the plan, just like the map you see when you walk into a mall.
4. If you share no other section with outside readers, share this one. It should be very clear and self-contained; it might be hard for you to tell if you have met these goals without getting outside readers.

What Can Go Wrong?

The following is a list of common characteristics of flawed definition of plan sections:

1. Slow, wandering beginning: too general

Some plans start out with paragraph after paragraph of boiler-plate background information cut-and-pasted from a grant application. This is not a good strategy if you are trying to get readers engaged in your idea and clear about the plan. Instead, start with short, tight paragraphs that clearly lay out your plan.

2. Starts in the middle of things: too many details

Don't jump into the details before giving the overview. To avoid this problem, get outside readers to read for you—without giving them the executive summary—and see if they can explain the "big picture" to you after reading the definition of plan alone.

3. Complicated, dense prose; large blocks of text

Of all the sections, this one depends most on plain language. Common words and short declarative sentences help. Add examples or models to make your idea more concrete.

4. Readers have lots of questions at the end

At the end of this section an outside reader should be able to tell you what the plan is and basically how it works. If they can't, you need to rework the draft.

Building Your Definition of Plan

Because plans are so different, it's hard to provide a real template for the definition of plan. Here are some ideas to get you started. In all cases the answers depend a lot upon your having written other sections of the business plan already, so don't worry if you can't answer them now.

1. In no more than two paragraphs, describe the product or service you wish to provide.

2. Who will be the customers of your program? the demographics (age, socioeconomic, racial, etc. characteristics)? where do they live? what else characterizes them? Use specific, concrete terms.

3. List two objectives of your program. Then, what will have to happen for you to know you've met these objectives?

4. Count the number of words you use that are three or more syllables long. Cut most of them.

Chapter 5

Industry Analysis

In the industry analysis section you describe the business you will be entering and analyze how you fit among the many entities that address a part of a given problem. Other organizations across the country—potentially in both public and private sectors—are probably already working in the general area of your program. In writing this section, you want to learn about what has been happening in that general area and what is likely to happen in the future.

Looking at the Big Picture

In the private sector, the industry analysis section of a business plan is often very detailed. Decision makers in that world need to be convinced that the entrepreneur understands the market, and that the new idea has a chance in that market. Industry analysis reviews things such as the key players in different market niches, historical trends in the size of the market, how "mature" the market is, the number of key players in the market, and future trends. All these analyses are meant to help you figure out what is important for a plan in this area to succeed.

45

Imagine a plan to provide worksite wellness services in a rural county. Worksite wellness is an industry. Before you enter that industry, as a decision maker, you would want to know some things about it. Who are the big players in the industry where you are? What are the trends in the industry nationally? Is one kind of product dominating? What different models exist? What are the factors historically that seem to have a big impact on this market? How big is the market now? that is, how many companies of different sizes are actually paying money for worksite wellness? What things are likely to change in this market in the next several years? The answers to these questions make up your industry analysis.

A good industry analysis section makes clear why you would be entering the industry: what you have to offer and why a customer would want it over what's already available. Recently, a Management Academy team from Virginia wrote a plan to provide a fee-for-service domestic well water testing program. The program would include education about well water safety as well as practical guidance and referrals for homeowners whose wells turn out to be contaminated. As they describe in their industry analysis, they would be entering a "specialty industry" focusing on the private homeowner, whose wells are only required to be checked when the house is built and when it is sold. Just by describing the industry as it exists today, the plan illustrates why the new service will be welcome.

> In Virginia, there are approximately 108 laboratories certified and more than 100 out-of-state water laboratories are also approved to test water. Each laboratory sets its own prices for water testing as they respond to the increased demand for such services in recent years. For most of the commercial labs, private well water testing is a very small part of their overall workload. Thus, turnaround time averages two weeks and all the information provided to the client consists of a print out report of the test results with limited interpretation to make any sense of the scientific data.

This is a good example of the level of detail you would want to get in your industry analysis. In the example, the planners want to show that a new initiative can be effective if it can test the water less expensively, provide the results more quickly, and include more information and help than do the current practitioners in this field. In more familiar public health terms, there is an unmet need. There is also a "niche" in the market for the proposed new initiative.

Key Industry Success Factors

The "key success factor" is a very important concept in business planning. Key success factors are those things necessary (if not essential) for an endeavor to be successful. In your industry analysis, you are trying to learn what the key success factors are for businesses of your type—before you commit. Imagine that you want to open a burrito stand. You would want to know (and your financial backers would want to be sure you know) all the important things about such a business. The basic question is this: what makes some burrito stands successful and some burrito stands not? "Key success factors" are those things that separate the successful burrito stands from the bombs. Talk to someone in the industry and they will tell you that location is one of these key success factors: where your burrito stand is located will have a huge impact on its success. For your industry, location is a key success factor: location, by itself, can determine success or failure. So you'd better have a good location.

This is precisely the analysis you have to do for your public health business plan idea. First, you have to figure out what "industry" your plan fits into. Then you have to do some research—that is, make some phone calls, maybe read some articles—to make sure you know what the most important two or three things are in that industry, the things that can determine your success or failure. One of the first places you should look is online: every industry today has a national association, and every national association has a website.

Take a mobile dental clinic as an example. Many public health departments have them. What are the key success factors for dental clinics? What makes some dental clinics sustainable and some not? In our state, availability of a good dentist is at the top of the list. Dentists can be hard to find; without the dentist nothing can happen. Throughput is another key success factor. To run a sustainable dental clinic, you have to be able to move patients through the system quickly. If you can't get enough people in the dentist's chair each day, you can't pay the bills.

A clarifying note: a key success factor is not the same as an evaluation measure. Evaluation measures are targets to tell you whether a program is moving toward a goal. "Ninety-five percent of patients get sealant in year one" is an evaluation measure that, after you implement, would show that your dental clinic was doing a good job of prevention. You need to know your key success factors before you implement. Key success factors determine success or failure of the program *in advance*. What if you couldn't get a good dentist? No program. What if you couldn't limit no-show appointments? No program. Not enough kids to fill the mobile clinic? No program. No way to insure Medicaid revenue comes in regularly? No program. No ability to track outcomes? No program. These are key success factors. Not having any one of them would seriously limit, if not destroy, your ability to sustain your program.

One way to understand key success factors is to think about programs you know well. In retrospect it is often fairly easy to figure out two or three things that were important in making a program succeed or fail. Many people have experience with big IT projects, for instance: think of one or two from your organization's history, whether successful or not. Typically the same three factors will get listed. No end-user involvement: no success. No way to avoid dual-entry of data: no success. No long-term system support: no success. These are key success factors across the industry of information systems, in and out of public health. Knowing the key factors is step one. Later—in your operations section— you can explain how you will deal with them in your design.

A good way to identify key success factors is to look at programs that didn't have them, and thus failed. Looking for failures helps two ways. Looking at failures often makes the importance of a particular key success factor show up in stark relief. IT projects that launch without end-user input can explosively and expensively fail. The other benefit to analyzing failures, frankly, is that they are much more numerous. Limiting yourself to "best practices" research might take 90% of the data out of your vision. Failures are harder to find information about—for some reason, people are less interested in publicizing them—but the information is valuable and abundant if you dig a little bit.

How to Conduct Industry Analysis

Your research methods for the industry analysis will depend on the nature of your program. Know the appropriate national trade associations and use them as a resource. In the case described earlier, the team depended on the Water Quality Association for information about the industry, trends, challenges, and current knowledge on the topic of well water testing and service. They also identified the regulatory agency responsible for well water in their state and were able to put their services in the context of required testing and standards. Often your best asset in all of this is your telephone and your network of colleagues locally, state-wide, and across the country. You need to talk to people who are doing it, or who have done it in different or similar ways to the way you propose.

We recently had a Management Academy team very early in the planning process, stumped about how to raise money for a mobile rabies inoculation program. Everyone they went to for funding was more interested in funding projects that had a clear human benefactor. On the one hand, they could re-pitch their effort to emphasize the risk of rabies to humans; on the other hand, they could make a phone call to a veterinary school and ask a researcher or practitioner: Where do you go when you need money for your work? They could also call veterinarians and see what they thought was essential for such a program. They were trying to raise money for a van, but is a van necessary? Could they use a smaller vehicle, or try to find indoor sites to visit and have pet owners visit them? One of the many groups nationwide that have established mobile units for other health programs may also have opinions about that—what size vehicle is ideal, what are the downsides of going mobile, what they have learned from their experience? Again, note that there are lots of underused and unused mobile units sitting in municipal parking lots. Why? What happened to the initiatives that purchased those mobile units?

The best business plans have this level of specificity about how things will really work. In our experience, the best way to get to that level is to talk to people who are doing the work you plan to do. Call them. Site-visit them. See how it works firsthand. Don't be shy.

What Can Go Wrong?

There are two things that most commonly go wrong in the industry analysis sections of public health business plans we read.

1. Choose the wrong industry to analyze:

It takes some good conceptual thinking to figure out what "industry" your idea inhabits, especially in public health. When in doubt, analyze as many industries as makes sense. The defining question is this: "Could learning about this industry help us see key success factors for our program?" One way to identify industry areas is to think about who might be competing with your program, and work backward to their industry. As you'll learn in the chapter on competition, it is common for new entrepreneurs—in any sector—to say "we have no competition." Rest assured that you do. If you truly have no competitors, it almost always means that you also have no customers.

2. Fail to identify key success factors:

"Identify key success factors" is the business world's way of saying, "Do evidence-based planning." You already do this very well. Public health scientists and practitioners work hard to understand what works (and doesn't), and why. You're wasting time if you don't use that information. And, be very specific: you are generally better off understanding the nuances of success factors than thinking about them in vague terms.

Building Your Industry Analysis Section

1. In what "industry(ies)" does your program fit?

2. Who do you know who knows this industry?

Name   Contact Info

_____   _____

_____   _____

_____   _____

_____   _____

3. Who are the big players nationally in this industry?

4. What are the three key success factors in this industry?

5. What are the main types of initiatives in this industry?

6. What major trends might affect this industry in the next several years? Consider economic trends, demographic trends, public policy trends, technology trends.

Chapter 6

Demonstration of Need and Target Market

W e have good news if you're in public health: one of the first steps in business planning—assessment—happens to be one of your three essential services. The ability to demonstrate need among a particular target market is a key success factor in business planning. You demonstrate need by examining the demographics of your community, identifying risk groups, and looking at trends in this population and the larger environment, all with an eye toward developing programs that will be exactly what the community needs.

Needs assessment is the foundation of all good business plans. The function of the standard business plan is to figure out how to meet a need in a particular population in such a way that revenues exceed expenses. Step one is to accurately describe and understand that need. That is exactly what good public health organizations do for fun.

Demonstration of need and target market are sometimes separate sections of a public health business plan and sometimes lumped together. We treat them together here because they both depend upon the same assessment activities for their data. We also deal in this chapter with assessing the larger environmental trends affecting the need and shaping your business plan.

Business Planning versus Strategic Planning

Before we continue, we should be clear: business planning is different from strategic planning. Most public health organizations have strategic plans. Many have quality improvement plans. You may use a Baldrige quality model, a state-specific quality model, or a quality improvement process such as APEX-PH (Assessment Protocol for Excellence) that's specific to public health. Many organizations use the National Performance Standards model from CDC. Some states, including North Carolina, are developing state accreditation processes for public health. You may use a community health planning process such as MAPP (Mobilizing for Action through Planning and Partnerships). These processes, and the documents generated through them, are designed to help an organization—or a whole community—improve effectiveness and establish priority areas. Many of these documents include input from stakeholders across the public health system, not just the public health department. The goal of these efforts is to stay on top of the community's health status and strengths and gaps in the public health systems in order to continuously set priorities, formulate goals, and based on that information, determine action steps. These are broad, organization-wide efforts.

The business plan, in contrast, is a very narrow document. As we've said, your business plan should describe one new venture in detail. It does not replace or restate your strategic plan. Instead it responds to one action step coming out of your strategic plan: "*We should address [diabetes, physical activity, flu]*." Your business plan does not replace your community health assessment, or your assessment of community themes and strengths; it responds to one part of those assessments that concluded "*People [in X group or neighborhood] see a need for [diabetes support, physical activity, flu prevention]*." Your business plan focuses down, in great detail, on the specifics of that one need and one specific idea for addressing it.

So, the business plan may expand on one lone action step from your strategic plan, and it might draw on or expand assessment data in one or more of your existing strategy/assessment documents. Existing assessment documents should help you establish the need for your new venture. You will want to connect your business plan to these assessments in order to show that you are working within existing priorities. There may be multiple existing assessments at various levels—local, regional, state, and even national—that relate to your particular business plan idea. Use the health assessments that are germane. But don't stop there. You will probably need to gather more specific data when you have a specific business plan in mind, for a specific audience.

Using Assessment for Business Planning

Assessing and demonstrating need are not unique to public sector or nonprofit business planning. Private-sector organizations obsessively assess consumer needs. Of course for some entrepreneurs, "needs" is a relative term: some of the needs they serve look more like "desires" or "whims" to those of us in the public and nonprofit sectors. When companies address the "need" for t-shirts that change color, or deep-fried Twinkies, or $500 per ounce perfume, or four-wheel drive vehicles for drivers who will never go off-road, they mean "need" in the broad sense of something that consumers are willing to spend their money on. Even if they don't really need it, if people buy it, there is a market for it. In other words, these companies can validate their needs assessment (or not) based on the financial results of their business.[1]

You recognize that the situation is different in the public sector. You may not know that, increasingly, the situation is different in the private sector as well. Not all for-profits share the one-sided view of "needs" we attribute to some. Many for-profit organizations seek other kinds of results besides shareholder return and are at pains to show how socially and environmentally responsible they are. Companies like Ben & Jerry's Ice Cream, or Timberland shoes, or Patagonia, are a few that have been very high profile about their interest in results beyond shareholder return. Many, many other companies have built on this idea.[2] You probably know of businesses and entrepreneurs in your own communities who fit this alternative mold: entrepreneurs who are acutely aware of broader community needs. Business schools now see strong demand for courses on sustainable business practices—business practices that return community value as well as shareholder value by eliminating environmentally and socially destructive processes.

So today, for many private-sector entrepreneurs, the bar is a bit higher in determining what needs get priority. That's certainly true of public-sector entrepreneurs like you. First, you are often spending public money in trying to give people what they need and want, so it is important to be sure that the need is real. Second, you're attempting to protect the public's health and safety—and the threats are many. So, assessment is just as critical in public health business planning as it is in all the other types of planning you do for your public health work. Your assessment of need has to confirm that the need is both real and compelling.

Again, some of you will want to dismiss the way business assesses need as different from or antithetical to the way public health does. Before you dismiss the private-sector model of assessing need, though, admit that the public sector is not immune from spending precious resources on programs that are either unimportant or ineffective. A good public health business plan process should prevent both problems. First, your business plan should demonstrate to decision makers and key stakeholders that your new venture is important: the need is compelling. Second, your business plan should show that the new venture will be effective (more about that in the chapters to come).

Using the Data

Say you know, through extensive strategic planning and community assessment, that the workforce in Virginia needs to address risk factors for heart disease, and you want to set up a program that provides preventive care in the workplace. First, you have to analyze and understand the components of the need, and what groups have what needs. You also have to show that your method of addressing this problem will be effective and efficient.

In your business plan you will want to get to the specifics of your claim about health need, which may be based on ongoing strategic planning and assessment of community health status more broadly. You want to go deep enough to show that you understand the problem in *your unique community* and understand it *in your unique target population.*

It's easy to get broad statistics for Americans from CDC, national organizations around specific health topics, or from health grant-making organizations. It is important, though—and usually more difficult—to assess need in the specific places and for the populations you serve. Start by defining that population:

- Geographically (for example, by zip code, county, size)
- Demographically (e.g., elderly low-income in area; unemployed; working people; single parents)

Then, if you can, find the numbers that prove there is a problem within your target area. If you happen to work in Virginia, you're lucky to have the Virginia Atlas of Community Health, launched through the Virginia Center for Health Communities in 2003. The Atlas is a web-based application that includes more than 120 population, economic, and health indicators for each of the 887 Virginia zip codes.[3]

The following example shows the type of detail ideal for making a good case.

Virginia Department of Health (VDH) statistics show the death rates for cardiovascular and cerebrovascular disease, malignant neoplasm, and diabetes to be 50% to over 100% higher in Wythe and Bland Counties than the statewide average. The following VDH table illustrates these numbers.

Disease Death Rate/100,000	Bland Co.	Wythe Co.	State
Cardiovascular (heart) disease	373.0	297.0	198.9
Malignant neoplasm	201.0	218.0	185.4
Cerebrovascular disease (stroke)	57.4	93.1	53.0
Diabetes mellitus	43.1	71.6	21.4

Once you've clarified the health problem to be addressed, you can show evidence that your way of solving it will work for this population. Let's continue the example, which aims to provide health screenings and education at worksites.

> Preventative healthcare screenings can reduce the cost of long-term care of diseases. Medical literature shows that early and episodic intervention prevents more costly or injurious disease progression. In the workplace, these effects range from a worker needing time away from the workplace for follow-up treatment to the total loss of ability to sustain productivity. Therefore, employers stand to lose skilled workers, incur lower productivity and recognize reduced profitability due to the workforce health status.

You also have to show that that need is not being met, or not being met efficiently or effectively. If other programs are attempting to address this need, what are they doing wrong? Are they not big enough? Are they run inefficiently or do they have some fatal flaw? Your research should show why clients aren't benefiting from current services. The following describes a health district's attempts to respond to a need, and the insufficiency of that attempt.

> The Mount Rogers Health District Wellness Team has responded to 11 of the 68 industries that have requested wellness screening for their employees over the past fifteen years. The screenings generally entail height/weight, cholesterol, blood pressure, PSA, and blood sugar....[However], these screenings contribute to the concept that the employees are receiving some level of health care, but few are actually receiving care and the services are not adequately coordinated.

Compare the benefits of funding this project to the costs of failing to fund it. Think about tangible and intangible benefits of implementing your project, that is, *tangible* cost savings, and *intangible* better community contact through partnerships, or improved worker morale. As much as possible, use data directly relevant to your community, state, or population. Many planners focus too broadly—at the national or even international level—and don't make as strong a case about the community in which they actually want to establish a program. It may be impossible to find local data that's as clean and robust as state and national data, but the public health problem you're trying to solve has a local dimension that you need to understand the best you can.

The Environment

Trends and forces in the broader environment—which includes political, economic, and sociodemographic factors—affect whether you will be successful. Understanding these factors will help you formulate the content and tack of your plan.

For example, political trends affect funding priorities every day. If your local politicians are getting pressure to develop policies against illegal immigration, that might impact how you roll out your Spanish-language (or other foreign language) health clinic. Political opposition may have nothing to do with what you've assessed with regard to need and the industry, and everything to do with the next election. Similarly, opposition might have to do with economic pressures—recent budget cuts, an economic downturn that has tightened the purse strings of potential community partners, or politically motivated spending priorities.

Your environmental assessment might inform your planning in a variety of ways. For instance, your assessment of the economy in your community will impact how you construct your budget. Can you expect start-up money from your county or municipality, or will you have to look elsewhere due to recent economic forecasts? Is your local factory experiencing a boom in business, such that it would share the costs of a workplace wellness program? Or are they expecting to be laying off workers and cutting benefits in the near future? What are rental rates in your area? Would it be better to rent space or buy it for the new program? What are competitive salaries? How fast are salaries growing (or not)? Knowing these details will fill in the blanks of your start-up and operations budget.

Assessing sociodemographic trends will inform your choice of target market. Is unemployment rising in your community? Are you dealing with a growing number of uninsured? Is your community aging, or do you have a high birth rate (or both)? Are ethnic groups in your community highly identified with particular places of worship (with which you could establish partnerships)? Is your population growing? Which part of it? Ideally, your organization is keeping tabs on these types of trends in its regular planning and assessment activities. Use your understanding of them to plan your program, develop your budget, and make your case to partners and other stakeholders.

The answers to these questions will tell you where to focus your energies. It may also tell you much about the political environment. If unemployment is falling, business owners may want or need to employ undocumented immigrants and may apply political pressure to serve this community. Growing rates of uninsurance may mean more people use the emergency room for routine care, causing the local hospital to be willing to collaborate on a solution or apply political pressure as well.

Although you cannot control environmental issues directly, if you accurately assess them, you can work with them. Think imaginatively about these trends, and see how they can help you create the perfect program for your community and see it succeed. If the environment is not warm to immigrants, what community partners could you work with to make the program more palatable politically? Could you situate it at a workplace, or a school, so that you reach the intended population at a neutral place? Chapter 10, which talks about barriers, deals further with ways to work around obstacles, including environmental ones.

What Can Go Wrong?

Public health professionals are generally pretty good at assessing and demonstrating need. Here's one main problem we see in Management Academy business plans: data are too general.

Most teams get that the needs should be supported with data. The path of least resistance is to settle for the data you can get easily. The easy-to-get data is not necessarily the right data.

This problem manifests itself in various ways and places. Some teams aren't able to find local data, so they extrapolate from huge state or national figures down to their local level. Fight the urge to write the words "local data are not available." You will need local information throughout the business plan. Look harder, look in different places, create your own, change your assumptions about what counts as data. Without knowing the nature of the need, you can't customize your program to deliver the right stuff. Without knowing where the need is, you can't target your program to the right people. Without knowing the scope of the need, you may not be able to build a compelling case, recruit partners, or estimate revenue potential. Keep digging.

What to Do with It All

You are never really done with assessment, because things are continuously changing, and as they change new challenges—and opportunities—arise.

If you keep on top of it all, you'll find it much easier to get started the next time you go to write a business plan for the next idea on your list.

Building Your Demonstration of Need and Target Market Section(s)

1. What are the three highest priorities of your organization?

2. What particular need do you want to address with this program?

3. Where does this need exist?

   a. Age of target?

   b. Gender?

   c. Geographical location?

   d. Socioeconomic?

   e. Other?

4. How do you know the need exists?

5. What else is being done (by you or by others) to address this problem?

6. How will your program be different from existing programs, or how does it build upon existing programs?

References

1. Collins, Jim. *Good to Great and the Social Sectors. A monograph to accompany Good to Great: Why Some Companies Make the Leap...and Others Don't.* Boulder, CO: Jim Collins, 2005.

2. *Fast Company* magazine keeps track of those companies it finds most interesting and innovative. See www.fastcompany.com (accessed September 26, 2007).

3. Wilson, Jeffrey L. Developing a Web-based data mining application to impact community health improvement initiatives: The Virginia Atlas of Community Health. *Journal of Public Health Management and Practice* (12: 5): 475–479.

Chapter 7

Competitors and Partners

This chapter outlines the section of your business plan about competitors and partners. These two terms will require some definition. If you are in public health, the concept of competition will likely be foreign to your day-to-day work, and might be a little frightening. In the business world, the concept of "partnership" is similarly frightening. To start with, let's try to demystify the terminology.

What Does "Competition" Mean in Public Health?

A critical part of any private-sector business plan is the section on competition, as you might expect—but what is the "competition" for a public health project? We often hear project teams say, "We're public health. Our project doesn't have any competition. In fact, we aren't allowed to compete."

By "we aren't allowed to compete" they really mean the following: "our projects aren't allowed to duplicate an existing service." That's commonplace in public health and perfectly sensible. But "not duplicating" is very different from "not competing." We mean competition in a much broader sense. The question is not about duplication; the question is, what other options do your potential customers have to meet the need you have identified?

So your "competitors" are the other people in the marketplace serving a need related to the one you intend to address. The challenge for you in this section of your business plan is to understand broadly what sort of "market" you are trying to enter, who else is already there, and who might be coming in the future. In virtually every case you will find that you are trying to improve upon what's already available to fill a need for a specific group. In other words: competition, but not duplication.

An example from the private sector will help clarify this point. Imagine writing a business plan for a movie theater. You've decided to show artsy movies, because no one in town shows them. You might very well think, as many business planners think, "We don't have any competition." But even if your town theater currently shows only blockbusters, you have plenty of competition. You aren't *duplicating* the other theater, but you will be *competing* nonetheless. You might try to avoid competing head to head, by aiming for a different segment of the "movie-goer" audience, but your target audience of movie-goers probably does attend movies at the other theater: the more artsy of the blockbusters, for instance, or blockbusters with artsy directors.

But that's not all. You will also be competing with other entertainment options: the local video store, Netflix, cable TV, maybe the public library, and the high school sports teams. And the better you do in business, the more the existing theater will be persuaded to show some artsy movies itself.

People like entertainment, and they believe they need it to be happy; lots of entrepreneurs have guessed or figured out what types of entertainment people like. As a result, your potential customers have many choices. These choices don't duplicate each other—although one might replace another. That's competition.

Another quick example. Bottled water—evidently, based on its popularity—fills a need for consumers for something quick and portable that quenches their thirst and seems to be good for you. Bottled water competes for customers with lots of other drink options, from soda-pop to sports drinks to milk, for instance. Bottled water isn't duplicating those other options. It is subtly different. Can bottled water replace other options? Yes, people sometimes choose a bottle of water instead of a can of soda, or a box of juice... or a glass of tap water. Does that mean municipal water systems are actually competing with beverage companies like Coca-Cola (which sells Dasani) and Pepsi (which sells Aquafina)? Yes. Customers frequently have choices in a marketplace. Beverage consumers have many choices regarding flavor, packaging, taste, healthiness, and more.

The same is true for most any public health project you will try: your customers will have choices. From this perspective, public health programs "compete" all the time. These days, many public health projects are trying to encourage healthy behavior—to the exclusion of other, less healthy options. So, an after-school program that encourages nonathletic kids to exercise at the Y, for instance, competes with a whole range of options, from the "couch potato" option (Nickelodeon, Nintendo) to the shopping option or the starting-a-garage-band option. These different options occupy different areas, have different prices, target different groups; the point is to know that market. Your workout program certainly doesn't duplicate Nintendo, but it definitely is going to compete with it. Any kind of "investors" or funders of a new program are going to be happier if they know you've figured out who the competitors are, what share of the market they control, and where your new business will fit in.

Some public health programs compete (and avoid duplication) by offering services in a niche of a market that isn't occupied by existing organizations. For instance, think of a flu shot clinic for a specific audience or geographic area that isn't being served by other providers, or a worksite wellness program for small companies that don't provide health insurance benefits. The idea is for public health to expand access to services not already being offered.

Private-sector planners actually do the same thing. They analyze the competition as part of their environmental scan, and most will craft a business plan that "runs to space": that is, it tries to find areas of a market that are not already occupied. So, even though they are "allowed" to compete, many prefer not to. The concept is similar to public health programs avoiding duplication of services. Public health departments would not want to start a new dental screening project if other sectors or agencies were already providing that service to the people who needed it. Private-sector entrepreneurs are also usually not interested in duplicating a service that already exists. It isn't fun and isn't likely to make you much money either.

To avoid the risks of competition, good private-sector business planners analyze the business environment they plan to enter in terms of who the competitors are, what customers those competitors target, how much market share they have, what they are likely to do next, and what their product costs—either in terms of actual price or other "costs," such as inconvenience or lack of access. In response to this analysis, planners try to make a different product, a better product, or a less costly product. It is just as important for nonprofit and government sector planners to understand where their "competition" is for a new venture. Don't see any competitors yet? Broaden your analysis until you see some.

A team from the first year of the Management Academy provides an example of the importance of breadth in scope—and in time—when considering competition. The team was writing a plan to provide wastewater treatment to low-income residents in a rural part of Virginia. No other entity provided this service, but the team rightly saw two competitors. The first was "the status quo," which is to say the ease, low cost, and tradition in the community of simply discharging untreated wastewater into the local creek. This competition the team planned to address with education about adverse health and environmental effects of raw sewage, as well as information about new statutory environmental requirements that were going into effect. Second, looking forward, the team projected that future competition might include municipal sewage systems being extended to the area. They recognized the need to plan ahead by creating an inexpensive, effective alternative that would offer residents a viable choice.

The key takeaway messages for this section: until you identify the competitors, you haven't fully understood the environment.

Competitors Can Become Partners

In public health business planning, an analysis of potential competitors serves a complicated dual role. In addition to identifying potential challenges in your intended market, this analysis should also help you find potential partners with whom you can ally your project. Thus the "competition" analysis becomes a partner analysis: How can existing players in the market help you achieve your objectives? How can you help them achieve their objectives?

Think of the "healthy behaviors" example we discussed earlier. Your competitor analysis might suggest that you should seek an alliance with the yoga studio and the running club if you share similar goals and values. In the wastewater treatment case, the municipal government welcomed the chance to partner with companies that could provide low-cost, efficient wastewater treatment.

In some ways this makes your business planning easier, although it doesn't make your competitor analysis any easier. You have to not only understand the market, but also be able to find appropriate partners based on the competitor analysis you do. More on this later.

Barriers to Entry

This section is about two related concepts. First, how hard is it going to be for you to break into the market you are proposing to enter? The flip side of that question is equally important: how easy is it going to be for somebody else to break into the business next month (and potentially take your business away)?

Barriers to entry come in many different flavors. Entering a business might require permission of some kind; it might require lots of cash; it might require specific expertise. For instance, in order to open a contractor's shop, or open a clinic, or open a restaurant, you have to get licensed. How big a barrier is getting the license in your industry? Your plans might face similar hurdles (although as government employees you may be the hurdle). Similarly, some markets require lots of expertise—a barrier that tends to keep new competitors out. Laboratory-based businesses tend to require space, specialized equipment, and science expertise that are difficult to obtain, for instance. Your plan should demonstrate first that you know what these barriers are, and second that you can get over them gracefully.

Note that it is not necessarily bad news when you find barriers to entry. A recent Management Academy business plan proposes to do water testing for residential wells in a rural district of Virginia. The barriers to entry into the water testing business have to do with expertise, laboratory space, and licensure. As a public health agency, this team easily clears those barriers. The existence of the barriers ironically makes the success of their plan more likely, because new competitors will find it difficult to enter the market.

Conversely, you can imagine another kind of business that requires no licensure, no major expertise, and little cash: for instance, a recent plan submitted that proposes to fit respirator masks to hospital employees. The designers of this service recognized that the barriers to entry into the market were very low. That makes their implementation easier on the front end, but makes their ability to compete long term more difficult. The low barrier means almost anyone could decide to offer the same service.

Other barriers have to do with the market analysis you have been building. If other competitors have already saturated and divided up the market, this can be a big barrier to new entries. In general, public health business plans should not go where others have already addressed the need effectively.

Identifying Competitors and Partners

Our advice for identifying competitors or partners is to start broadly. Ask who in your community has a stake in this particular health issue or geographic area. Who has some stake in the health of this particular population? Who has interest or expertise in the specific kind of goods or services you are considering? This section of the business plan encourages you to analyze all the possible competition to whatever behavior change you are trying to create, and further encourages you to take advantage of opportunities to partner with like-minded organizations.

Let's go over an example to show how this section of your business plan builds on prior sections, such as your industry analysis section, and how it might work to identify competition and partnering opportunities as well. Think of the dental van example: in Chapter 1 we shared the outline of a dental van business plan. These vans are not uncommon across the country. The need for such a plan is clear: providing dental care and prevention services to underserved school-age children can greatly improve overall health for kids. The need for access to dental care is acute in some areas (including rural North Carolina) where few dentists live, and fewer have space for Medicaid patients. A project such as this represents an opportunity to do solid public health: first and most important, it creates access to an important service; and second, it creates an opportunity to do low-cost, high-yield prevention work that will prevent costly interventions later.

Where access to care is the problem, you might reasonably conclude that "competitors" are not an important worry. The "run to space" strategy is designed to minimize competition. This dental van project is a classic example: the need is created by the fact that there are no dentists in the area serving kids on Medicaid. Kids who need dental care don't have an option (except going without care).

At this point, put on your 4-D glasses and add the "sustainability" dimension to your analysis. The fourth dimension is time. Markets change. How long will the market stay as it is today? In this case, you might try to answer a range of questions: first, what would happen if the supply of dentists changed? What if more dentists showed up? Well, that could change things—but it doesn't seem likely to happen. What would happen if reimbursements changed? That may be unlikely in the short term, but it is hardly unimaginable. Higher Medicaid reimbursements—or changes in how other non-Medicaid patients get reimbursed for dental care—could change the market. Perhaps in the future local dentists will decide that they do want Medicaid patients after all. In fact, as a public health leader you might well support that policy change to improve overall public health impact!

Based on this analysis, success seems to depend on integration with local dentists. Any dental project needs a dentist to do the work: attracting and retaining a good dentist are very important "success factors" for these projects (along with retaining quality assistants, who won't stay if the dentist is difficult to work with). The support of other local dentists is also critically important, because they are in a position to help you in important ways. They can help by accepting referrals for work that can't be done in the mobile unit; they can support the program politically; they can offer professional support if you hire a dentist from the outside; they can refer people to your service. Long term, your relationship with the local dentists might be critically important if the market changes.

Your competitors section should make this sort of analysis, in very specific terms. Who are the local dentists, by name? What parts of the market does each serve? Which ones serve children? Which ones take Medicaid? How will they react if you enter the market? How might they benefit if the program is successful? Based on this analysis, lay out the plan for communicating and integrating. How would we prefer to integrate with them in the start-up phase? How will we integrate with them for referrals back and forth? How will we integrate with them in the longer term? The more specific you get here, the better. Your plan looks more feasible if you can describe the environment in detail and outline exactly what local dentists are willing and able to do for you. Ask individual dentists or a professional group to write a letter in support of your project, describing their role in it. Decision makers and potential funders want that level of detail to assure them that a big resource bet will in fact pay off.

You will have other partners in a project like this one. For any project having to do with children, the schools are potentially a make-or-break partner that can make sure the service is delivered to the population that needs it. Again, make a detailed analysis. Who are the key stakeholders in the school system? Who at the district level will need to support the project? At the school level you might need both administrators and school health nurse support. You might need faculty support to ensure success, especially if students will be pulled out of classes. Your program could be seen as competing with other school programs: your business plan should outline what programs those are. How will your program avoid conflicts with other enrichment or health initiatives in the school? If you can, get a letter of support from a local school leader.

Thinking Strategically About Partners

We have talked extensively in this book thus far about the value of partners in creating and protecting the health of the public. You almost certainly have examples from your own work in public health. Partners are important for what they bring to a project: expertise, money, space, equipment, access to a population of customers, energy, political clout. Some are important—like the dentists in the previous example—because of what they could do to you if they became displeased. Successful public health entrepreneurs think carefully about what they need to succeed, and pick their partners accordingly.

The following example comes from a team planning a "Safety Village"—a planned learning facility to provide hands-on exercises and walk-through safety exhibits for children. With an eye toward strategic partnership, they included representatives from the county health department and city and county fire departments on their team, and looked toward a local nonprofit organization to which the team members also belonged.

Partners in Safety

The Safety Village's primary partner will be Life and Safety Education Resources (LASER). This nonprofit 501(c)3 organization was formed by a coalition of local health and safety advocates, emergency services personnel, and community leaders. LASER's mission is to reduce injuries, death, and property damage to the citizens of Wilmington, North Carolina, and New Hanover County, North Carolina, and in the Cape Fear area of North Carolina.

Southeastern North Carolina has many organizations such as fire services, law enforcement, and public health, with highly qualified staff that provide and promote safety awareness and injury prevention education. What has been identified as missing is a mechanism by which to bring the various safety partners together and combine these valuable resources and skills. This role will be filled by LASER.

The plan goes on to name specific potential local, state, and national partners (including the names of current leaders of these organizations), as well as local competitors that target similar markets. For each of the organizations you list here in your plan, be they competitor or partner, include a description of the organization and its product or service offering, and how the program will fit in with your goals and objectives.

As the example illustrates, describe what your partners will do for your program in very specific terms. What role will they play? Have they got experience with this type of activity that you can point to in order to assure your stakeholders that these partners are good additions to the team? Do you have any evidence that your community and/or organization are ripe for this type of alliance (especially if it hasn't been done before)? How long are the different partners to be involved? Include your partners in the planning of your program and the writing of your business plan, so you have accurate, precise answers to these questions.

Why Partnerships Matter

Partnerships serve your purposes for a lot of different reasons. Clearly, in the current economic climate, it's good to have a lot of resources, not only financial but also brainpower resources, to come at problems and their solutions from different angles. Partners can provide practical things like space and infrastructure. Some partners—especially those you haven't worked with before—can provide more abstract things, like a consumer-oriented mindset, and the skills to make that mindset a reality. In addition to new mindsets, new nontraditional partners can become conduits to networks you never knew existed.

As we've intimated before, *partnership* is a common term in public health but has some negative connotations for some in the business world. In general businesses prefer the term *strategic alliance*. A strategic alliance is a partnership with a specific purpose and clear roles and responsibilities, scope, and time horizons. Thinking in terms of strategic alliances may help you provide this type of specificity and avoid the common problems of "partnership fatigue" (where you burn out your partner by going to them too often) and the echo-chamber effect (where you don't hear anything from your old partners that you didn't already know from the last time you worked together).

A partnership (or a strategic alliance) is hard to describe in the abstract. It is different from a "negotiation," although it can require the type of flexibility and communication skills necessary for working out a deal; it's clearly not "human resource management," although it takes a lot of the same skills to manage partnerships as it does to manage individuals in the workplace. Forming and using a strategic alliance is a multifaceted leadership skill that requires networking skills, analytical skills, strategy skills, political skills, negotiation skills, and more.

Creating and maintaining alliances with nongovernmental organizations is also an important way of maintaining power in the community. Public health professionals are often seen as "honest brokers" in the community. You have the power to bring people together in ways you might not have thought of because of your position of authority in matters of the public's health and safety. One of our Management Academy graduates put it this way: "By acting entrepreneurially, exercising leadership and good 'followership,' and seeking strategic alliances with others in the community, public health agencies can use their authority to add value in a way no other entity can."[1]

This particular graduate, the Director of the Cumberland Plateau Health District in Virginia, went on after leaving the Management Academy to be part of creating a Regional Health Information Organization (RHIO). This coalition of over 80 individuals from over 30 organizations—including health care providers, insurers, employers, and other community leaders—undertook a two-year strategic planning process of needs assessment, research, and consensus-building to address coordination of care issues. They developed a system, called CareSpark, to communicate and share health information and data among regional providers, to enable coordination of care and public health improvement. As we write, CareSpark is creating a sustainable structure for the electronic exchange of health information in Virginia. The technical challenges for such an undertaking are demanding, but the human challenges prove more daunting because many of the organizations involved were, essentially, competitors. But they became partners under the leadership of public health.

The partnering activity of the Cumberland Plateau Health District is a case in point for the power of thinking in broad terms about working together across disciplines to solve public health problems. In one case, the Management Academy team from Cumberland Plateau in 2000 worked with pharmaceutical companies to create a plan for providing and managing free pharmaceuticals programs from various manufacturers to the benefit of low-income patients. In another case, a coalition led by the Cumberland Plateau Health District and community mental health leaders and including leaders in local government, economic development, education, law enforcement, the judiciary, and health care, is working on a plan to combat the multifaceted and troubling crisis of methamphetamine drug abuse.

In yet another example, the Cumberland Plateau Health District created both the Mountain Empire Public Health Emergency Coordination Council and a spin-off organization, the Mountain Media Public Safety Council. Their goal was to coordinate public health emergencies better and engage the media for both greater public health and safety coverage and crisis communication. These organizations are clearinghouses for decision makers and provide key support to people in health agencies in three neighboring states and a neutral meeting ground to foster mutual understanding and communication between public safety agencies and the local media.

In a final example (there are more), another alliance led by the Cumberland Plateau Health District is OneCare, a nonprofit referral network for human and health services in the southwest region of Virginia. This coalition of health, social service, community assistance, and related entities has adopted the Healthy People 2010 goal of 100% access and 0% disparities. OneCare has allied itself with the Virginia Economic Bridge, a business, economic, and workforce development consortium, and shares with it an executive director.

We list all these programs at the risk of going on too long about one health district; public health managers around the country have stories like these. The point is to show the effect of thinking differently about the role of public health leaders, and the value of regular extra-agency longitudinal relationships in benchmarking, trust, communication, and cooperation for the public good. For one thing, such varied groups bring in a broader range of ideas of the possible—governmental public health managers are not used to thinking about 100% success, while business leaders might not have thought before about the effect of health on their workforce and consumer base.

You might ask, how does the Cumberland Plateau Health District have time to do all these things—and still provide the basic services to their population? First of all, this is a way of providing the services they are obligated to provide. They're just bringing in more hands and minds and spreading the work around. But second, sometimes a partner is just the thing to provide sustainability, in the form of an entity that will take over operations after a set amount of time. But more about that in Chapter 11.

What Can Go Wrong?

As we've noted, a common problem among public health and private-sector business plans is the inability to recognize competitors. If you don't see any competitors, it virtually always means one of two things, both of them bad:

1. You don't see competitors because you are viewing things too narrowly.

Solution: Change the way you are thinking about the market you want to enter. Get out of your own perspective and into the perspective of your target market for an hour, or a day. Make a phone call or a site visit to adjust your view. Be an anthropologist for a little while, studying your target market. What options are currently available to your desired customer? What are your customers doing instead of coming to you? Consult with people who are good at brainstorming and who know your audience. Read a book on innovation.

2. You don't see competitors because there are no customers.

This is potentially much worse than the first problem. If you are trying to generate revenue, it means somebody, somewhere, is going to have to want what you are providing enough to pay for it. If there are no competitors, it is possible that no one wants the customers you are willing to serve, but it is more likely that there is no market. If your state does not require an emissions test, for example, that explains why car-care companies are not providing emissions testing to motorists. A plan to sell emissions testing to motorists is not likely to succeed in this market: individual motorists see no need for that service.

Beyond not recognizing competition, some plans are inadequate for another reason:

3. Insufficient specifics on how and why partners interact.

A common shortcoming we see in the Competitor/Partner Analysis is when planners neglect to plan for the operation of a partnership. Especially if you partner with businesses—but even if you partner with other agencies—it is important to understand and articulate the shared objectives and specific roles of different partners. Too many "partnerships" never progress beyond the stage of planning meetings together. Make it clear what the different partners will give, and what they will get, out of a relationship. Is your "partner" providing materials, money, space, expertise? Or just moral support? Spell out the details. Get it in writing and put the letter of understanding in your appendix.

The idea of partnering is one of those topics that Management Academy alumni come back to again and again as an example of how their "whole outlook has changed." Expanding your idea of competition and partnership is one of the fundamental ways to change your thinking that generates huge benefits.

Building Your Partners/Competitors Section

1. List the other entities that offer the type of product or service you plan to offer.

2. Which of these might be a potential partner, and what might they offer?

Potential Partner	Contact Info.	What they offer

3. What regulations, requirements, or other conditions make it challenging to do what you want to do?

4. Page 65 of *this chapter* has a list of questions specifically related to planning a dental van. Create a list of similar questions specific to *your* plan. Write the questions (say, 10) here:

1. _____
2. _____
3. _____
4. _____
5. _____
6. _____

7. _____

8. _____

9. _____

10. _____

5. Now, answer them!

6. What will the partners you identify do in the start-up phase? What will they do in the sustainability phase, after the program is started up and is running smoothly? (complete for each partner)

Partner   _____

Roles in Start-up:

_____

_____

_____

Roles in Sustainability:

_____

_____

_____

References

1   Unpublished correspondence, John Dreyzehner, April, 2006.

Chapter **8**

Marketing

G ot ads? Most businesses do. As American consumers, we're adept at recognizing advertising, and we understand basically how it works. But there's much more to marketing than making up clever ads.

The essence of marketing is research—something public health managers already understand and do well. The classic message given to first-year marketing students is this: assume at the outset that you know nothing about your customer. First, you must collect information about them, then you must modify how you plan to market based on what you learn. Marketing class in business schools also starts with the four P's: product, pricing, place, and promotions. All four of these parts go into how a product is presented to customers in a marketplace; marketing is about how that presentation is crafted.

Why a Marketing Section?

Marketing campaigns don't necessarily require a business plan. Public health business plans, though, can benefit from marketing principles. You should have a section that describes how you plan to "sell" your program.

You already understand the basics of promotions. You have already thought about what your product is. If you work in public health, you may well have studied or heard about "social marketing," the type of marketing that designs messages to shape health behavior. This chapter will take you through the basics of the standard marketing plan, and then discuss the additional wrinkles involved in marketing a public health venture.

The Four P's

The four P's—product, pricing, place, and promotions—define how you will sell something to somebody in "the market." You might think of the four P's as asking four key questions. Product: what are you selling? Price: for how much? Place: where? Promotions: how? The marketing section of your business plan is partly about the *answers* to these questions—but it is primarily concerned with who is *asking* the questions. In other words, who are your customers?

Customers are implicit in all of the "four P" questions. You are selling something to a group or groups of customers. Based on your needs assessment work, you already have an idea of who your target market is. In this section of the business plan, you want to analyze that target market. Who are they? What do they need? Where do they shop? What choices do they make? What do they care about? What motivates them? Are they ready to make the choices you want them to make? How much are they willing or able to pay?

Let's think about a "jail health" project as an example. Imagine a project to provide preventive health services to inmates in the county jail. The target market seems obvious: inmates. But who are they exactly? Demographics of this group should be easy to find (yours might be more difficult). For this example, imagine that they are male, mostly between 18 and 34, with above-average rates of smoking and IV drug use. Your target market information plus your needs assessment should fit with the services ("product") you have decided to offer. Prenatal care might not make sense here.

"Price" is a relatively new concept in public health circles. Price is of course an integral part of a product or service. In the private sector, entrepreneurs have to decide whether to be the high-price exclusive option (like Mercedes-Benz), or the low-price value option (like Kia), or somewhere in the middle. In this case, you are a public agency and so is the customer—we wouldn't expect the inmates themselves to pay for their health screenings; they will be paid for by the correctional facility. So, the product and pricing probably ought to be on the value end. And regardless of who is paying the bill, it is necessary to know how many units you can expect to provide, and how much each costs you, so that you can decide how much to charge to cover expenses. We cover this topic in more detail in Chapter 12, Financial Planning.

"Place" is where you sell your product and offer your service. In this example, place seems pretty settled for us—we know where they are, and they aren't leaving for a while. On the other hand, depending on the level of security, they do have some choice about what they do with their time in jail, and where they spend it. Within a specific jail, where can you attract positive attention to your offerings, and where can you offer them so that they are difficult to avoid?

"Promotion" is a little complicated. The target seems to be inmates, and indeed that's who has been identified by your needs assessment. But your target market includes other, critically important people. Jail staff will have a huge impact on the success or failure of your project. The marketing for the service should be directed to the jail operators as much as, if not more than, the inmates, since inmates are generally not in control of the services they receive. What do we know about this additional target market? Who are they? What do they need? What do they care about? What would convince them to participate? This concept of "marketing" to those who have the power to accept, support, or fund an initiative is very important, and success at this is closely related to the feasibility of a project.

This jail health example comes from a Management Academy team from several years ago. The marketing section of their business plan addressed their plan for "promotion" to decision makers in this way:

> To target the Jail administration, the marketing strategy will be to create presentations documenting their responsibilities for the health of the inmates, recent shortfalls in meeting these responsibilities, and ways the county health department can help them alleviate these shortfalls. The focus will be both on the legal ramifications of their not addressing these problems and on the health department's unique ability to provide low-cost testing and care at the Jail and the ways the Jail could use the health department's specialty clinics, including the HIV Clinic and TB Services.

This is a strategy for selling the jail health concept to decision makers. It is different from a *social marketing* strategy that might aim to convince people to take the preventive health tests and therapies the program will offer. This team's plan for that included posters in the jail workout room and in other common areas, with a message associating health with strength. The jail administrators were also seen as instrumental in encouraging participation.

The jail health care program was implemented. The idea was good, and indeed, their "sell" to the jail was easy because of legal pressure pushing the jail in their direction. The county political leadership was behind the plan because the county government would ultimately be financially responsible for correcting the health care situation in the jail.

Most planners, however, do not have the luxury of threatened legal action forcing their market to choose and pay for their service! Even in the case where there is a law forcing people to do something, it usually takes real marketing to get them on board. The readers of your marketing plan want to know you have thought through your strategy, to ensure that you don't waste time with false starts and misdirected energy while searching for an appropriate way to sell your product.

How Will You Reach Your Customers?

As we said at the beginning: assume you do not know your customers, and learn as much about them as you can to plan your marketing strategy. In the private sector, planners try to answer three key questions in analyzing a marketplace. The first question is about numbers. How many people are there in your market? Note the potential overlap with the needs assessment you may already have done. As we know in public health, needs change: what might the future market be, in three years, six years, ten years? The second question is about segments. Within the market, what groups can you identify? The assumption is that certain groups might be preferable for you to target: you might pick the largest group, the group most in need, the group most open to your program, the group that's easiest to reach, once you know what the groups are. The third question is about the desires of your target group. What do they need? What do they want? What do they like and dislike? How do they see the problem?

So, your strategy will be different in obvious and not-so-obvious ways as you try to reach different groups—county jail inmates vs. their administrators, versus parents of toddlers, versus high school students, for example. If possible, identify a key leader who can help shape the decision making of their peers: beauticians to talk about mammograms or other screening tests; physicians to convince other physicians to raise questions about patients' activity levels, for example. These people will "speak the language" of their colleagues and may be more effective than a "specialist" coming in. Similarly, if you're trying to reach new immigrants, you should distribute your material in their language as well as English. Parents are more apt to go to PTA meetings than to rock concerts; teens might feel more comfortable in a mall than at a health department. Baby boomers and retirees read newspapers; under-40s read email; students read Facebook. These are all stereotypes, but like all stereotypes they have some basis in reality. Professional marketers spend a lot of time figuring out sensible categories into which groups of customers fit, then find out where and how people in each category like to receive messages.

Selling Ideas with Social Marketing

Social marketing is using marketing principles to influence people to change their *behavior*. When we talk about social marketing, we generally mean "selling" an idea to people whose behavior—and ultimately health outcomes—you'd like to change. Social marketing, then, has a broader focus than standard marketing—although a businessperson would say he or she, too, is trying to change people's behavior (so they'll buy their product) and is also working at the population level (so everyone will buy their product).

Your marketing strategy will be directed toward the people whose behavior you would like to make more healthy or safe or those who have responsibility for their health decisions, such as parents or other caretakers. Your thinking about it should involve deciding who your primary customers are and how best to reach them, and knowing who or what is competing with you in reaching these customers.

Focusing Your Message

After describing the market(s) for the product, your plan's marketing strategy section should identify the *focus* of the messages to these markets. Usually, there are several different ways to focus your message, depending on what you believe will convince the audience. For example, a campaign to get more people to use seat belts will have to decide whether to focus the marketing on the safety gained by wearing a belt or on the legal ramifications of not wearing a seatbelt. In North Carolina, planners decided the public already knew they'd be safer with seat belts, but didn't care. They did care about getting a ticket. Therefore, the campaign focused on legal consequences rather than health benefits. The focus on the law, in the "Click-It or Ticket" campaign, was extremely effective, whereas earlier campaigns based on public safety were not.

So, you must decide: if you're trying to get teenagers to stop smoking, do you focus on the message that they'll die sooner if they smoke—at age 70, for example, rather than 80? Or is it more effective to send the message that smoking may cause the face to show wrinkles at age 25 rather than 45? With parents, you might use messages about second-hand smoke's effect on children, but such messages would probably be less effective with teenagers. And, unlike the preceding seat belt use example, to dissuade 20-something men from using illegal drugs, reminding them of the law against drug use might be less effective than giving them information on possible impotence caused by drug use. If you know what your market segment cares about and believes in, you can focus your message more effectively.

See how in the following example, gleaned from a plan to provide training and certification in emergency preparedness to child care centers, planners understand and articulate appropriate targets for marketing their program:

> Due to the nature of the program, there will be a two-tiered marketing approach. The target populations include (1) [decision makers at] the child care facilities and (2) the parents or guardians who employ their services. Due to the differences among these two populations, the marketing focus will be different for each group.

Although the plan is ultimately to benefit children, children are not the targets of the marketing plan because they are not independent actors in matters of their care or protection in emergency situations. This plan goes on to define the different markets in terms of the focus of each of the different strategies:

> The program will be marketed toward child care facility administrators as a method to promote their facilities' readiness to respond in the best interests of their clients in an emergency. This strategy will focus on the benefits in being prepared for an emergency, including presentations at various child care industry events and program task force meetings, the dissemination of educational materials to facilities via mail, and promotion on a dedicated Web site.
>
> The goal with regard to parents will be to increase parental awareness of the importance of child care emergency preparedness and the benefit of using a certified child care facility. This includes the development of a dedicated Web site with FAQs regarding risks, certification, a listing of certified facilities, and a brochure containing similar information for distribution to parents/guardians at various public sites and at participating child care facilities. In addition, a mass media campaign (e.g., public service announcements, spots on local radio and television shows, newspaper articles, and fliers) will be launched with a notable and widely recognized spokesperson to emphasize the importance of the preparedness certification. Care will be taken so that the public and parents and guardians of children in child care facilities are not alarmed, but rather their awareness and market expectations are raised.

Note how this example details a multipronged plan going forward, as well as the logic behind the plan.

Social Marketing and the Four P's

Social marketing professionals talk about the four P's too:

- Create an enticing *product* (the package of health—and other—benefits associated with the desired action).
- Minimize the *price* the target audience must pay or believes it must pay in the exchange for this healthier behavior.
- Make the exchange and its opportunities available in *places*

that reach the audience and fit its lifestyles.

▨ *Promote* the exchange opportunity with creativity and through channels and tactics that maximize desired responses.

Some of our Management Academy students balk at the second of these items, "price," reminding us that the governmental health community is rarely in charge of how much its services cost. But, if you're going to have a solid plan, you still have to know how much it costs because somehow it has to be paid for. Moreover, in social marketing, "cost" is not limited to a financial price tag: sometimes your customers are "buying" a behavior change. For example, if a drug user changes her behavior and stops sharing needles with her friends, she may lose those friends (think of what would happen if you told your husband or wife you could no longer hold hands, due to health concerns). That is a cost to her, and something to think about when attempting to market a clean needle intervention.

Finally, as we've noted before, public health programs may be supported by people other than just the final "customer," so the marketing plan may have different levels: one for customers and one for funders. Decision makers considering a needle exchange program might think about the "cost" in public perception, whether the public might think they're encouraging criminal behavior, for example. Your marketing plan may have to address such perceptions as well.

Know Your Competition

We talked about knowing your competition in Chapter 7, when we discussed who might see your new endeavor as a threat or rival for their customers. When it comes to social marketing, knowing your competition has to do with knowing what other "products" your customers might choose over yours. These may be the anti-action that you're trying to stop:

▨ Smoking over not smoking
▨ Having sex over remaining abstinent until marriage

Your competition may be "cheaper"—it could actually cost less financially, as in using unsafe materials over safe ones at a building site, or cost less socially, as in sharing needles rather than insulting fellow drug users by insisting on clean ones. Your goal in your marketing campaign will be to convince them of the value—in lives saved, safety maintained, integrity, laws followed, the positive perception of their peers—of undertaking the more "expensive" activity.

Your competition may be easier:

▨ Easy paint removal over more complicated, but safer, lead abatement methods
▨ Watching TV over undertaking more vigorous activities

Your competition may seem better for other reasons:

- Fast food over fresh vegetables (fast food may be less expensive, and easier, as well)
- Traditional fun parks versus a "safety village" designed to educate children about safety
- Driving to work versus walking or taking public transportation

Your marketing strategies should directly address these competitors: don't ignore them, for your audience is not ignoring them. If your market segment thinks it is easier to drive than take the bus, don't focus your marketing only on how much gas they'll save, or how much cars pollute. You'll be more effective if you focus at least in part on how easy and convenient the bus really is, perhaps including the testimonials of professionals who have "made the switch."

Other Ways to Understand Behavior Change

Another way to talk about behavior change is through the "stage of change" theory, which deals with peoples' readiness to alter their behavior. According to the theory, there are five stages of change: precontemplation (haven't thought about changing yet); contemplation (thinking about changing the behavior); preparation (willing to change); action (changing the behavior); and confirmation (succeeding in changing the behavior).[1]

In the childcare center preparedness program plan described earlier, parents of young children may not yet have contemplated choosing a childcare center certified in emergency preparedness procedures. Thus, it would not do any good to begin with messages about how to find certified centers, and the first stage of marketing is planned to focus on educating parents about the prevalence of emergencies—how many natural emergencies may be expected to occur, what types of man-made emergencies might affect their children, and why preparation for these events is important. Information about what would be involved in a certification process might then be appropriate so that when they've absorbed these messages they will be ready to change their behavior in regard to this issue and advocate with their own child's caretaker or choose one that has received training and been certified. Focus group or other market research could tell you where your market segments are in regard to your topic and give you insight into where you want to start your efforts.

Another important part of some social marketing activities is the addressing of normative beliefs in the target population. A normative belief is a social perception, or norm, that individuals or groups hold as true and use to dictate their actions. Examples of normative beliefs that affect health behavior include "smoking makes people look cool" (if I quit, I'll be unpopular); "everyone else is drinking every night" (so if I want to be sociable, I should, too); "women shouldn't initiate talk about contraception" (so I'll just hope my boyfriend carries a condom); "only young (or old) women get breast cancer" (so I won't get a mammogram); "real men don't get sick" (so I won't go to the doctor for regular check-ups).

Normative beliefs are often very strongly held and difficult to change. When you know the true corollary to a false normative belief, however, you can use it to change behavior, or at least cause people to think about their behavioral choices. Smoking actually makes you look prematurely old (not to mention that it ruins your health); people of all ages and both sexes get sick with cancer and other preventable or treatable conditions. It's not actually true that everyone else is drinking on college campuses.

The lesson is clear: know your audience. Get detailed knowledge of what your audience thinks and cares about. Four key elements of your plan—product, place, price, and promotions—rely heavily on your knowledge of the target audiences for your product or service.

What Can Go Wrong?

We make planning your marketing strategy look easy. Indeed, writing the marketing strategy section of your business plan is pretty easy: a lot of it is common sense. But when you come to implement that plan, you might come up against some stumbling blocks:

1. Rose-colored assumptions

Otherwise practical people sometimes overestimate the demand for their product and the ability of their marketing plans to sway their target market. If you think you will achieve 100% market penetration with a new initiative, think about fluoridated water. Fluoridation is by some accounts a nearly perfect public health intervention: it is cheap, population-based, effective, virtually risk-free, and requires no behavior change at all on the part of the consumer. Yet CDC reports that only two thirds of the U.S. population with public water receives fluoridated water.[2] The lesson is that even the best interventions don't reach 100% of the market. In general, we suggest that you be practical, conservative about demand for your product, and very specific about who you will target; then be realistic about how many in your target market will respond.

2. Changes in how marketing approaches work

Marketing is harder than it looks. American society is awash in marketing messages, so we feel like experts on the subject. But we've also all heard lots of electric guitar solos: that doesn't make us Santana. Marketing is hard, and it is getting harder. The marketing environment is changing rapidly. Marketing strategies that worked well ten or fifteen years ago no longer work, partly because people have developed resistance, due to having been exposed to so many marketing messages so often. In general, the declarative mass-media approach works less well than it used to, which means that public health mainstays like flyers and brochures are getting less and less effective over time. By contrast, grassroots-based marketing approaches seem to be more popular and effective. The lesson here is to involve partners in designing and executing the marketing plan. The best marketing plans tend to be diverse and incorporate plenty of direct contact with customers in the design and execution phase.

If you work to know your audience, create a product they need and will use, and educate yourself about what will work to reach them with your message, you will have an effective marketing plan.

Building Your Marketing Section

1. Succinctly describe the "product" you are planning to offer.

2. To whom do you plan to offer it?

3. What are the key characteristics of your target market(s)?

4. Who else will have a stake in your plan and/or need it "sold" to them?

5. Describe the types of messages that might best reach your target audiences and why.

6. Describe the media you plan to use and why.

References

1. Prochaska, JO, Redding, CA, and Evers, KE. Transtheoretical model and stages of change. In Glanz, K, Rimer, BK, and Lewis, FM, eds., *Health Behavior and Health Education: Theory, Research and Practice.* San Francisco: Jossey-Bass; 1997:60–84.

2. National Oral Health Surveillance System. Retrieved on September 19, 2007, from http://apps.nccd.cdc.gov/nohss/FluoridationV.asp.

Project Operations

U nlike a traditional private-sector business plan, your plan will not be judged by profits, but by the efficiency with which you can meet the public health goals you've shown are so important. Your purpose in describing operations is to show that the plan will be efficient and effective. Efficient: you will meet the goals quickly, without wasted effort, and make the most of the available resources in the community. Effective: the time and effort and other resources you put in will result in the maximum delivery of health.

Up to this point in the business plan, you have analyzed the needs, the market, and the environment very carefully. The project operations you design will simply respond to what you found in your environmental analysis. This is a key section: it links the environmental analysis you've done with the resources you hope to use (coming up in the finance chapter).

More than some other sections, this section has two equally important audiences. This section should be directed to both decision makers (the people who will say "go" or "no-go") and to future managers of the program you are describing. This section should be specific enough and clear enough that it can function as a how-to guide for running the project once you implement. It should have enough detail so that you could give it to someone else and they could implement it. Those specifics will also have to convince decision makers that your design will work as you say it will.

General Organizational Overview

At the start of this section, it's a good idea to describe your organization as it exists now so that you can show how the organization will integrate the new program. Most of you will write business plans for programs that fit into a larger organization. Implementation will depend on fit.

A full organizational assessment will not necessarily find a place in your written plan, but it will inform much of your planning in the long and short term. Ask some of these questions: What are your organization's strengths? The identifiable weaknesses? How is your organization structured? What are the tasks and responsibilities of the staff? How are individuals compensated, and will compensation be sufficient for new tasks and responsibilities? This type of assessment helps outline the assets you have in place internally that can help your plan succeed. It may indicate where the organization needs to change something or learn something in order to implement your program— or how you need to adjust your program to the existing reality. It may show where you need help from a partner.

An important question to ask when beginning to plan your program is, who are the key individuals in your organization whose support or buy-in you need most? Who are the highly respected, influential people everyone else will follow? It is important to convince these people first so that they'll lead the way.

Human Resources

In this section, you will describe the people power needed to run your program. What will your human resources and staffing needs be? What role will each staff member have in the new program? What experience/training/skills will they need in order to perform their duties? The introductory paragraph might outline the status of your organization now, its current strengths and foreseen needs, as in the following example:

> This plan will exist within an already successful public health department with strong leadership and organizational structure.

Utilities, space, technology support, management support, and supervision are already in place.

It is a good strategy to begin by recognizing the foundation on which you will build a new program (gleaned from your organizational overview). This particular business plan starts that way, and then goes on to describe how the organizational structure and personnel will have to change with the new program:

> The program will require the creation of a new Behavioral Health Section of the Buncombe County Health Center. The newly created section will operate under the existing Primary Care/Clinical Services Division. The new Behavioral Health Supervisor will report to the Medical Director and Director of Patient Services and will supervise the therapists.

Include (in the text or in an appendix) an organizational chart with any new divisions or personnel noted. In the text, be as detailed as possible about the responsibilities to be given to program personnel, as well as the time they will spend on the program, in terms of FTEs (full-time equivalents). Think ahead to when your program expands, and how staff will expand to meet new demands going forward. Do you need to allow for calculated growth? Discuss the diversity of your staff, how you will maintain or create it, and why it may be important.

HR and Organizational Culture

The concept of "human resources" is broader than just "the full-time equivalents (FTEs) I need for this project." When it comes to people, the whole is greater than the individual parts. Ideally, you thought about your human resource needs as an organization—both in its narrow sense of individual people and its broad sense of organizational culture, values, and mission—long before now. If you had anything to do with hiring, you chose people if not for the new roles you're now planning for them, at least with the mutual understanding that they may have new roles and responsibilities some day. You have, ideally, communicated to them your organizational goals, and they share your vision for how to reach those goals.

You might want to describe your organization's culture and how that culture will affect your project. What does your current organizational culture look like? Where will your current organizational culture be helpful (or not) in rolling out this new project? Answering these questions will help you decide what steps to put into your plan to make success more likely. Think about the unity of direction in your organization—is everyone on board with the strategic direction that underlies this new project? How is the morale? Will a new project put pressure on current staff? How could that pressure be eased? These questions help you find potential barriers in advance and strategize solutions. Is your organization good at delegating tasks? How empowered do the employees in your organization feel? What has to happen in your organization to implement change? What leadership resources would assist in making change work for your organization? These questions help you think about who needs to be involved, at what level, to smooth the road toward implementation.

Our general advice here is to communicate with your colleagues about your plan. Some years ago, we had a team write a great plan to develop a website where restaurant owners could go for information about state health and safety rules and regulations, training offerings for their employees, and other resources. When describing operations, they "volunteered" another office within their own organization, writing, "The Office of Environmental Services will play a critical role in the development and ongoing maintenance of the website." Unfortunately, no one told the Office of Environmental Services they would play this "critical role." No one from that office had been invited to join the Management Academy team. This lapse occurred partly because when the team was formed they were considering a different plan altogether. Still, the lesson is clear: get critical people on board early, by communicating with them and soliciting their input for planning. Writing someone into the operations section suggests that you have discussed the plan with them in advance, negotiated the amount of time needed over some duration, aligned the goals of your plan with the existing goals for that part of the organization.

You should communicate with people below you *and above you* on the organizational chart about your plan. We hear from Management Academy graduates all the time about how they "don't have the necessary organizational support" for their project. They go home from the Academy with a great business plan—an approach supported by the data, great partners in their pockets, a strategy for marketing and funding the plan—and it comes to nothing because the organization does not commit the time, or the staff, or the money to carry it off. We have a lot of data about business plan outcomes, and in summary, teams that don't implement their plans most often attribute that failure to lack of organizational support. Teams also name lack of time, staff, and money as factors. In other words, the plan lacks support from the powers that control the priorities of an organization.

This point is less about what you write in your plan and more about what you say about your plan, to whom, before you finish it. Scratch the surface of "lack of support" and usually you see a lack of communication during the planning stages. If "the boss" doesn't understand the project and, in fact, is not involved in its development, she will not—indeed, cannot—share your vision. And if she does not share your vision, she will not understand the need for resources. If you don't communicate effectively with the boss, the best you can hope for is that she will "let" you work on your project—as soon as you've done everything else on your list. Especially when you're considering a sea change in the way your organization does things—and introducing business planning methods and assumptions constitutes such a change for most public health departments—communication can make the difference between the success and abject failure of your plan.

Think of it this way. You are likely going to need one of these things to operationalize your plan: (1) new people; (2) new roles and responsibilities; (3) a whole new mindset; or (4) all of the above. None of these can be accommodated without support from above. So, before you go any further, go talk to your boss.

Before you go, think about your boss's priorities: your boss answers to a lot of stakeholders, is responsible for a large operation, and doesn't have time for plans that will fail. You need to know—and communicate—that your plan will succeed. The following is a list of characteristics of "plans that succeed" that we share with Management Academy students, and you might want to use it as a checklist before you go talk to your boss: Business plans that succeed are often *Testable* (you could do a pilot version); *Reversible* (can return to status quo); *Divisible* (can be implemented in stages); *Concrete* (they provide tangible results); *Integrated* (they cover sunk costs or otherwise build on existing programs and resources); *Familiar* (good models are available); *Congruent* (closely match goals); *Widely valued* (have publicity value that stakeholders will appreciate); *Marginal* (small and risk-free); *Idiosyncratic* (you can start it by yourself); and/or *Timely* (reacts to an emerging crisis or uses a new means of attacking an old problem). If you can attest to your plan's having these characteristics, then you're ready to talk to the boss, and you should do that before you go any further.

Really. Put the book down and go talk to your boss now.

Space

We encourage Management Academy students to think creatively about space when developing their plans. Don't think that just because you are creating a new program, you need to find offices and desks in your organization for the people who will be running it. You might, but you might not. Not having space can be a significant barrier for a lot of plans, so thinking creatively might help you implement and sustain your program. You could think about partners who could give in-kind space: this will have the added benefit of making your program easier to spin off if you wish to do so in the future. Consider programs that send people out into other spaces—on-site wellness programs for workplaces or schools, for example—or programs that use people who work from home— online training modules for restaurant workers' health and safety, or other "virtual" programs. Or, consider "down" times in the spaces you do have and how you could capitalize on underutilization by doubling up their use. Thinking flexibly about how to use space might help you minimize your program's space requirements.

Daily Operations

Your daily operations section includes detailed descriptions of everything that will need to be done to carry out the program. Write what the day-to-day manager of the future program will need to know. The big picture is to be sure you've addressed the "key success factors" identified earlier in your plan. The detail is important too: who is going to do what when?

For example, describe in detail the process for handling the program's financial requirements:

> The Town of Appalachia has agreed to bill for sewage service to Imboden residents. The Town currently bills Imboden residents for water usage and has a system in place to bill residents in other portions of the county who receive both public water and sewage, with the sewage portion of the bill equaling 100% of the water bill plus a $5 fee. The residents of Imboden have agreed to this rate. The Town of Appalachia has agreed to receive the monies and forward the amount received minus 5% administrative fee to the PSA monthly.

This lays out the details of who pays how much, who sends the bill, who receives the money, and how the money gets routed to the appropriate parties. Incidentally, the section makes clear that these details are already agreed upon by the appropriate parties.

Along these lines, and at this level of detail, describe how your new venture will operate. The basic challenge here is to describe who does what in order to create the product or service you are planning. You have already described the "who" part of the equation. Here, define as clearly as you can the work that your people will do. In addition to training and oversight—not to mention a paycheck and benefits— they may require other resources to get their jobs done: materials, equipment, space.

For example, in defining the technology and/or information systems that will be needed, consider the following:

- Personal computers: Who needs one? At what cost? What kind? With access to what external resources? Backed up and secured in what manner?

- Database: Who will design it? Who will maintain it? How will it be backed up and secured?
- Specialized software: How much will it cost? How long will it last? What will the upgrade cost? Will people need training to use it?
- Other technical machinery or equipment: Cost? Maintenance? Does it need a special power source? Require special safety measures?
- Internal capabilities of your organization in order to manage the technology (now and in the future)

A useful exercise in deciding what to include in your operations section is to consider the experience of an individual customer going through your program. The goal here is to think about what you will need to create the best possible program for the user. So often we get stuck thinking the other way around, customizing our program to the amount of money being offered by a grant, or the government, or some other sponsor. We scramble to spend money so it doesn't go away at the end of a grant or fiscal year. Or (more often) we cut corners, or are unrealistic about our needs during planning, because the funds are limited. In these situations, we can't think too much about the client's experience, because if we did we'd come up against the fact that their wait may be too long if we don't hire someone new to serve them; or our facilities are not going to be welcoming, or large enough, or appropriately outfitted, if we stay within the budget dictated by the external source.

Instead, think through operations from the customer's viewpoint. If you think honestly about what you really need to do the job right, and you do not flinch from those needs—just as private-sector business planners don't flinch from what they need when setting out—you will find a way to get them met.

Partner Roles and Logistics

Some Management Academy participants get caught up in this section listing all the stakeholders in their program. Only those partners who are actually involved in day-to-day operations of the program should be included here. "Partners" who are just mailing you a check, writing a support letter, or letting you come by to borrow second-hand supplies are not integral enough to your operations to be included in this section. A rule of thumb is that all partners appear in your competitors and partners section; only those involved with operations need to go in your operations section. These partners are really part of a strategic alliance: they all have clear roles to play, they commit resources, and they get some benefit in return.

So, for each partner, outline the roles and responsibilities that have been agreed upon. Describe how you plan to share control of the program, and how you plan to communicate among partners. This next example shows the type of detail desirable for describing the roles you and your partners will play:

> The Wise County Public Service Authority has agreed to monitor and maintain the system when it becomes operational. Tennessee Valley Authority will monitor water quality in Pigeon Creek quarterly for two years after the system becomes operational. Health department staff will monitor the quality of the treated effluent as it leaves the treatment plant prior to dispersal in the soil. The project manager will receive and evaluate reports from all monitoring activity.

Description of partner roles could come up in multiple sections of your operations section, depending on what they are going to do. For example, your partner might be providing evaluation assistance (often provided by partners in academia, for example), equipment or IT assistance, or space. Again, partner roles might change over time: describe the transition points.

Implementation Plan and Timeline

This is often a separate section of your business plan, but it is closely related to operations. This is where you present a detailed timeline with specific dates by which you expect to implement key actions or reach certain milestones. This plan should include milestones for getting the program up and running as well as for the operational phase of the plan. Often these milestones are listed as "number of people served," but you may have others depending on your plan. These milestones should be specific enough that it will be clear whether you have met your goals based on the timeline you lay out. Put what you've already done on the timeline if it makes you feel good: if nothing else, doing so will provide a record of everything that went into the project and help you when you start from scratch next time.

The timeline can be included in the text of your document, by organizing bullet lists of accomplishments under bold "by this date" headings, for example. It can be in table form, showing dates and steps and (ideally) a lead person. You can depict your implementation plan graphically using a spreadsheet such as Microsoft Excel (with shading to show the start and end of a task) or using specialized project management software that highlights decision points and critical events within a process flow. The key goal is to think carefully and in fine grain about the details that you (or someone) will have to take care of as the project starts up. If you are a manager, this will feel familiar. Who needs to do what, when?

The more detailed and specific you can be, the easier it will be for you to gauge your progress as you go. Timelines are especially useful as you bring new people on board in the implementation phase. The timeline allows planners to communicate forward in time with the implementation team. Ideally the timeline provides a one-glance summary of goals, strategy, tactics, and measures of success. Timelines in our culture are imbued with magical powers: many people believe (judging from their behavior at least) you can cause things to happen just by putting them on a timeline. Magical or not, a good timeline can be helpful.

Evaluation and Quality Improvement

We suggest your description of how you plan to evaluate your program should go in the project operations section. We strongly encourage you to involve evaluators in the design of your program. Any business needs to have feedback loops: you need a way to measure the quality of your product. Measuring quality is essential in public health business planning. What's more, measuring outcomes is essential in sustainability. Your evaluation section should plan for both of those needs.

Include the specific, quantifiable measures of success for your program—the health goals you hope to achieve, and the data collection that will show progress toward those goals. In addition to being quantifiable, each outcome measure should have a specific time period associated with it. Your project operations section should include a description of the "quality improvement" methods you will use to read these measures and make changes in your program to improve program outcomes.

Because we think evaluation is an important—and often neglected—part of program planning, we devote all of Chapter 10 to evaluation. The fact that you won't necessarily give evaluation its own section in the business plan doesn't mean it isn't important. In fact we think that a good business plan incorporates aspects of a good evaluation plan from the beginning to the end, from the design to the execution.

What Can Go Wrong?

1. Not enough detail

The dangers as you navigate the operations section are on the left side: that is, you are more likely to get in trouble on account of what's left out. In general, for this section, more detail is better. To write and edit this section, you want the help of good detail managers, the kind of people who ask lots of questions and figure out how things work. You want the kind of people who, when you go out to eat, think to ask on behalf of the vegetarians whether the rice is prepared with chicken broth, and who can also equitably divide up the bill and the tip afterward.

The details are important both for the decision makers and the implementers. Decision makers don't necessarily know whether all the details are right—but most are clever enough to notice when you don't have enough detail. If they find an inconsistency in the details, they may use that to judge your entire plan.

Implementers are a critical audience, and a critical resource. If you don't include front-line workers as you plan, you will certainly make mistakes on the details—and you will leave out details that these same workers will later discover, perhaps only when it is too late. "Oh, you didn't know that this machine was supposed to be anchored to the wall? Or that this door wasn't wide enough for a wheelchair? Or that this question on this evaluation form is illegal to ask? Sorry—I could have told you that."

Similarly important is to imagine and then describe exactly what the customer experience will be. This helps convince decision makers, align front-line workers, and clarify for yourself what background details will have to be worked out to provide that experience.

2. Not enough structure

Writing a detailed section such as this one requires that you impose a strict order on things. You want the reader to finish this section and think, "OK—everything is in order. They thought of everything, and everything is in its place." The feeling should be akin to walking into a big library, or a nice clean woodshop: lots of useful little parts are here, and you can find them because they have logical places!

You can create that orderly sense of detail by making good use of headings, organizing sections in a logical way, and using parallel structure. Your layout should reinforce the sense that the details have been arranged thoughtfully and comprehensively. Tables and timelines, pictures, organizational charts, and maps can help.

3. Short-sighted about staff needs

Two problems with regard to staff come up often. The first arises when the whole program depends on one staff member who is intimately involved in its development and implementation. That situation, of course, only works as long as that staff member is available. Maybe they get a promotion because of all the great work they've done. Maybe they move away, go on maternity leave, or just get a lot more responsibilities that make running your program untenable. The other problem related to staffing is when there's one key person needed for the program—the physician that's going to run a new HIV clinic, for example—but you haven't spent any time considering how to identify, recruit, and retain that person. How are you going to get a qualified professional to come to your rural (or inner-city, or suburban, for that matter) community and fill that role? You must consider this in your planning.

4. Overly optimistic in timelines

Freelance workers estimating the time it will take to do a project learn to estimate the number of hours and then double it. We say, just be realistic. It will take time to recruit staff (if you need to), it will take time to get customers, or furnish space, or carry out evaluations. If you're depending on a grant for start-up, know when the grant money will be disbursed, and plan around it. In general, things take more time than you think they will, so plan for that.

Plan to Continue Planning

Planning at the nuts and bolts level will inform other parts of this business plan, as well as plans you write in the future. For instance, without doing the work described here, you cannot construct a meaningful budget. You may also have better luck attracting partners if you can communicate clearly what they are committing to by joining you. And, when you go down this road again, you'll have basic facts at your fingertips—number of employees, the status of your organization's space, technological and other resources, the reasonableness of your time frame. You will have to update them every time, but you'll have a template.

Like a blueprint for building a house, however, your plan is a detailed, seemingly exhaustive description of what you're going to do—until you come across that boulder that affects where you can put that house, or the zoning law that affects its façade or the uses to which you can put it. Your business plan is essentially a theoretical document, pristine and perfect only until it comes up against barriers that affect whether and how you can move forward. Of course, your preliminary assessment work looked at laws and policies, political trends, and funding streams—but these may change and affect your plan in ways you can't see now. Ideally, your skill at planning the nuts and bolts of implementation will serve you as you look then for options for getting around any barriers that stand in your way. Chapter 11 takes the longer view of sustaining your program and getting around those inevitable boulders.

Building Your Operations Section

Human Resources

1. What specific number of FTEs will be needed for this program?

2. What training will be necessary for this program?

3. What addition(s) to the organizational chart will be necessary?

Communications

■ I have talked with my boss about this. S/he understands what we want to do and is supportive.

■ I have talked with my staff about this. They understand it and how it might affect them.

4. List any questions raised by your boss or staff.

Daily Operations

5. Describe the basics of daily operations: how will the program work on a typical day?

6. What supplies will be needed?

7. What space will be needed?

8. What else will be needed?

Partners

9. List the partners that will be involved in daily operations:

Name   Roles/Responsibilities

_____

_____

_____

_____

10. How do you plan to communicate with these partners?

Timeline

11. List the program's major milestones and an approximate "done by" date for each; as appropriate, include a person responsible.

Evaluation

12. What will be a "home run" for this program?

13. For more on evaluation, see Chapter 10 (Evaluation).

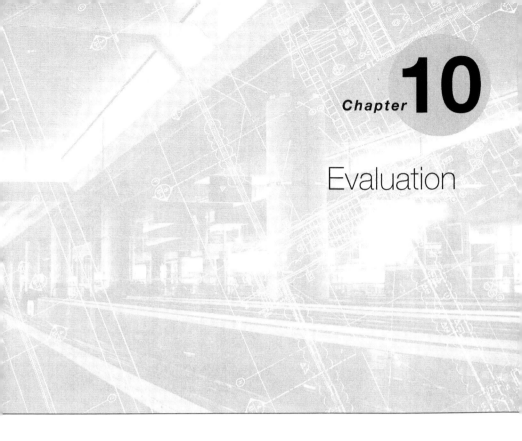

Evaluation

valuation is not a standard section in business plans. As we noted, in the private sector evaluation focuses on measuring for quality improvement. Typically the evaluation process gets described as part of the operations section of a private-sector business plan.

This isn't to say that evaluation is unimportant in the private sector: it is extremely important. Jim Collins, in his classic book *Good to Great*, argues that the ability to find the right measure of success is a key factor in separating great companies from the merely good.[1] In one sense, the private-sector business plan is in large part an evaluation plan, because return on investment is one of the key outcomes! Similarly, there are aspects of the typical evaluation plan woven throughout your public health business plan: assessing need, understanding the target market, developing measures of success, finding evidence-based solutions, collecting the data and using it for quality improvement, and ultimately using it to build energy for sustainability.

You may know how to do evaluations. Evaluation reports are typically required by granting organizations, and grants drive public health organizations. Like you, your funders are mission-driven: they need to know that their money is in fact contributing to their public health mission. Funding organizations adjust reporting requirements over time because they want to get the best value (in terms of mission) per dollar they spend. Accordingly, they ask grantees to measure things that demonstrate effectiveness and efficiency. Evaluation is also necessary if you want to base what you do on evidence. Evaluation provides evidence about *how* and *whether* something works.

We all know there's no point in continuing to do something that doesn't work, but we all know many organizations that do just that. A sound evaluation plan makes it possible to measure

1. the outcome you are trying to reach and
2. the process that leads to that outcome.

Once you've measured, you can learn and improve; you can share your positive results with others and use those positive results to attract more resources.

In at least some government settings, funding for evaluation is difficult to get; nonetheless, there is pressure to demonstrate "success," often in a short time frame. If you can systematically incorporate evaluation into your initial planning, you will have a better chance of getting the evaluation funded and getting the analysis done.

The detail and examples in this chapter will be useful in making evaluation an integral part of your project. We have tried to err on the side of giving you more detail than you need in order to write the business plan; we want to give you a sense of how to operationalize and use the evaluation plan after you implement your project, because that helps build sustainability (Chapter 11). In some cases, you may have stakeholders (funders, a board, partners) who want a separate evaluation plan; in some cases you might cover the key parts of the evaluation design and implementation in the course of writing your business plan. The important thing is to do the planning described here.

Why Evaluate?

Knowing how and whether your program works is responsible program management: it is a key responsibility of those who spend other people's money. Evaluation results help external and internal personnel understand "where the money went." Without evaluation, you cannot know whether to continue or discontinue a program, whether to design more programs like it, how to improve its quality as it matures—basically, you can't know much about where you're going now and where to go next unless you evaluate. Sponsors, including private foundations and governmental entities, require evaluation so that they can be assured that you are doing what you said you would do and that what you're doing makes a difference. The better your evaluation is, the more fodder you will have the next time you want money from those sponsors to start up a new program or expand an existing one.

Evaluation reflects good thinking—thinking that is logical and based on results, rather than intuitive and based on untested theories about what you imagine will work. And good thinking goes a long way toward designing a successful program.

The CDC Evaluation Framework delineates six steps for designing and implementing an evaluation and reporting results. The first three steps begin at the planning stage while the second three are the implementation steps:

1. Engage stakeholders
2. Describe the program
3. Focus the evaluation design
4. Gather credible evidence
5. Justify conclusions
6. Ensure use and share lessons learned

The following sections examine these steps in more detail, and outline how your evaluation plan might fit into your business plan.

Step 1: Engaging Stakeholders

For virtually any program in the public health sector, you will have multiple stakeholders: health is important to many, and responsibility for it is broadly shared. Stakeholders may include funding agencies, governmental officials, community members, participants, and program management and staff. Stakeholder support is typically critical to your success, so you should involve them in the planning and implementation of any evaluation. Their needs and desires for the program, their questions, and their perspectives should inform what you evaluate.

You can involve stakeholders in planning an evaluation in numerous ways. Funding agencies usually build evaluation expectations into their funding documents; their priorities are generally clear and straightforward. You can solicit input from community members or government officials through public forums, and from program participants through interviews or focus groups. Program management and staff are you and your colleagues. Their involvement is constant and highly valuable since their knowledge of the program is probably the most comprehensive of any stakeholder's. You may even want to consider "outsiders," those who oppose your program for whatever reason, or who do not have an interest in its continuation. Gathering their input could strengthen your evaluation and give it credibility as a comprehensive look at all perspectives. For best results, be concrete: ask stakeholders to define the successful outcomes they hope to see. Take three outcomes generated mutually, write them down, have everyone sign the sheet, laminate it, and stick it to the wall for all to see and acknowledge as the program goes forward. Use this document to tell you what to evaluate.

Clearly, the evaluation is analogous to the target market section of the business plan. Just as you do there, here you must think about what your program will mean to different people, what they will hope or expect to get out of it, and how you can make sure they are served.

Step 2: Describing the Program

To evaluate a program you must start by describing it. Program descriptions include the mission, objectives, and goals of the program; the strategies being used to reach these ends; and the results you hope to achieve. We've described a similar process in Chapter 4.

A basic logic model could help you with this description. A logic model is a picture of how a program works and what it is meant to accomplish. It displays the theory and assumptions behind the program, it shows how and in what order activities should occur, and it shows the links between resources, activities, and results. In most logic models, this information is depicted graphically. It may be useful as well to "tell the story" of how the program works. Give the story a human scale: tell about one person's experience. The point is to make sure that the logic of the program, the story of how it will work, actually makes sense.

Figure 10-1, from the W. K. Kellogg Foundation Logic Model Development Guide, shows the basic form of a logic model:

Here's what these terms mean:

1. **Resources/inputs** are the funding, partners, networks, staff, time, facilities, and policies that affect your program.
2. **Activities** are the processes, techniques, tools, actions of the program, products, services, and infrastructure.
3. **Outputs** are the direct results of program activities, usually described in terms of size and scope of services and products delivered or produced.
4. **Outcomes** are specific changes in the target group, including changes in attitudes, behaviors, knowledge, skills, level of functioning, etc.
5. **Impacts** are organizational, community, or system level changes that result from program activities.

Basically, your planned work includes resources/inputs and activities; your intended results include outputs, outcomes, and impacts. Creating a logic model and sharing it with stakeholders, particularly program staff, facilitates evaluation planning because it represents a shared understanding of what the program is designed to accomplish.

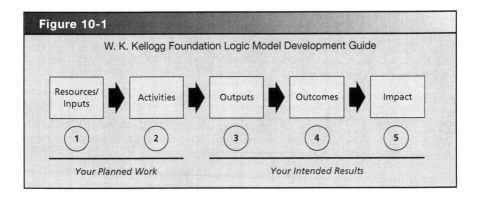

Figure 10-1

W. K. Kellogg Foundation Logic Model Development Guide

Resources/Inputs → Activities → Outputs → Outcomes → Impact

1   2   3   4   5

Your Planned Work   *Your Intended Results*

A Word About Outcomes

You notice that in the preceding list of outcomes we do not list changes in population health status. Of course improving the health of your target population is the long-term goal of any health care or public health organization. Decreased numbers of heart attacks, tooth decay, cases of flu; increased years of life, children who swim safely, adults who have drug-free lives—we have plenty of desired outcomes. Some of your stakeholders will want you to give them this "gold standard" of health outcomes, but you cannot. There are just too many variables affecting people's health at the population level to measure this type of outcome and trace it back definitively to your program. What you can measure is how people eat, what access they have to dental care, whether they get flu shots; you can measure what they know about exercise, water safety, drug laws, and healthy personal choices. You can measure how many smoke, or get mammography exams, and you can attribute improvements in these rates to your program, if appropriate. Some individuals affected by your program will definitely improve their own health status in measurable ways. Over time—a long time—you may be able to see health status outcomes at the population level. At least in the short term, though, you will have to resist the pressure to look for ties between one program and overall population health improvements.

The lesson for your business plan is this: make your outcome targets few (one or two is best), feasible, and short term. "0% disparities, 100% access" is a great vision: it is unambiguous and galvanizing for a nation. It is not a feasible outcome for your business plan to achieve in a five-year time period. You want an outcome big enough that it represents a challenge, and big enough that reaching it would clearly confirm your success. At the end of five years, what single thing would convince all the stakeholders that the program was a success? Janet Porter, COO at Dana-Farber Cancer Institute and founding co-PI on the original

Management Academy grant, always boils it down by asking, "What is a home run?" So, ask yourself: at the end of five years, what will we consider a "home run" for this project?

Step 3: Focusing the Evaluation Design

It's not too hard to learn what your stakeholders care about. Funding agencies will tell you up front, customers will tell you if you give them questionnaires or invite them to take part in focus groups, and your colleagues who are running programs will tell you, if you ask them.

Often various stakeholder groups will have more evaluation questions to be answered than there are resources for gathering their answers. You must set priorities among the various questions.

Here at the Management Academy, we come across this problem often. Our own experience may be instructive. Our stakeholders include four original funders and a fifth organization that managed the process; one current grant funder, the CDC; state-level customers who pay for slots in the program; local customers (hundreds of public health professionals from around the country); these professionals' professional organizations, the National Association for County and City Health Officials (NACCHO) and the Association for State and Territorial Health Officials (ASTHO); the UNC School of Public Health and its practice arm, the North Carolina Institute for Public Health; the Kenan-Flagler Business School and its practice arm, the Kenan Institute; and our staff. Our original funders are still interested in our mission and want to know if we're succeeding in building organizational strength so that they can perhaps fund new programs on the same model; our future customers want to know the program works; our graduates want to convince their colleagues to come and want to know the success stories of other graduates; our parent organizations want us to continue to bring executive education to professionals nationwide every year; our staff want to know whether the program they are working on will be changed or discontinued. Many different users, and uses, of evaluation data.

Look for overlap, look for utility, and prioritize. As our Management Academy program evaluators say, "It is preferable to answer a few questions thoroughly than to answer many questions poorly." They also say, "Gathering information that no one will use is poor project management." In other words, ask only the important questions that will be of use to the program.

The questions raised by stakeholders might come to you in broad, vague terms. A funder or partner might want to know, "Was the program popular?" A staff member might want to know "Was the service easy to use?" "Did it work?" "How can it be better?" A customer might wonder, "Can it be done less expensively?" or, "Will you be expanding?" Many of these questions can't be answered in concrete terms because they are too abstract. Your first job is to determine what focus areas these questions are in—that is, do they refer to the "inputs" end of your logic model (how much did it cost, was staff sufficient?); or implementation (how long were appointment times, how many people were served?); or the "outcomes" end (were intended changes achieved?)?

Evaluation questions will also move across focus areas of the logic model over time. During program planning and initial implementation (Years 1 and 2), the focus will be on inputs and activities. As the program matures, evaluation should examine outputs and outcomes (Years 3–5).

Step 4: Gathering Credible Evidence

For your business plan, it is important to have an idea of what evidence to gather, as laid out earlier, but you must also have a good process for gathering the good data.

Say you have a program like one that a Management Academy team devised to create peer health training. The team, from Dare County, North Carolina, got a grant to partner with a school system to train high school students; the high school students in turn taught middle school students about health and nutrition. The Institute for Public Health helped the team evaluate the program, known as "Peer Power."

The funding agency wanted to know whether middle schoolers' health behaviors changed due to the Peer Power program. You'd categorize this concern as an "outcome"-focused question. The funder could use the answer to demonstrate program effectiveness (justify their monetary commitment) and identify best practices for other grantees.

Ask what things you can measure to find the answer to your question. These things are called indicators. The acronym to describe the best indicators is SMART:

- Specific
- Measurable
- Action-oriented
- Realistic
- Time-limited

We broke the question "did middle schoolers' health behaviors change" into two more specific questions: "Did the program change middle school student self-reported physical activity behavior?" and "Did the program change middle school student self-reported eating behavior?" Indicators for these questions would be the number of middle school students who report physical activity three days a week, or the number of middle school students who report eating three to five vegetable servings a day. These indicators are *specific, measurable*, and oriented toward *action* on the part of the subject; it is *realistic* to think this measure might be moveable using this program; and, if you ask both before and after the program's implementation, they are *timed* to indicate the program caused (or was correlated with) the change. To measure the impact of the program further, students in a "control group" —who are not in the school system where the program is being implemented—could also be questioned. We recognized that asking them more than once might contaminate the second findings because you might have "educated" them—thus affected their behaviors—without meaning to.

Impacts are really just broader and longer-term outcomes, and have similar questions and indicators. To find out "How did the program impact the community," many indicators could be identified. One impact indicator might be the attitude of participating high school students about teaching as a career choice, which in this case was of interest to the health department. You could explore this question through focus groups of high school students. Another indicator could be high school student parents' opinions about how the program affected their children. Parent opinions could be measured through focus groups or structured interviews. You could also look at the community more broadly. Did the students involved with this program get involved independently in other programs, or expand the program beyond the planners' original parameters? It turns out they did. They developed their own innovative methods of reaching middle school students through their own version of "social marketing" around healthy behavior; they also got involved with a community drive to increase tobacco law compliance at local stores, and worked to increase the number of nonsmoking restaurants in the community. These impacts are measurable and may be of interest to community leaders, school system personnel, and funding partners. Although every one may not follow the SMART guidelines to the letter, you still want to make questions and indicators as precise as possible. This will allow you to be very specific and clear about your findings.

Beyond identifying indicators, gathering credible evidence has to do with choosing the appropriate sources for your information, making sure your data collection and analysis procedures are sound, and compiling enough evidence that you create confidence in the results (without overburdening respondents). Your evaluation plan should describe how and why you are choosing your sources (what perspectives you hope to get); your operations plan might include on the timeline tasks such as training your data collectors, creating data collection instruments, coding the data, and checking errors. Your appendix might include draft survey instruments or a description of the data management system.

Step 5: Justifying Your Conclusions

Conclusions must be justified in order to be accepted by stakeholders and others as reliable. Conclusions are justified when they are linked to the evidence gathered, they address the goals of the program as originally established by the stakeholders, and they can't be accounted for by alternative explanations. The Peer Power evaluation illustrates the point: middle schoolers' healthy behaviors increased measurably during the program. This is a "positive" finding based on the value of improving participants' health, and these findings cannot be attributed to other programs or conditions that affect subjects.

When preparing evaluation reports or presentations, address the limitations of your evaluation, as well as directions you might take in future evaluation of this program to address those limitations. How do these limitations affect the findings? Might other or more subjects be useful? What other elements of the program might fruitfully be examined? How might you address possible bias? In general, think about your audience and anticipate their questions and concerns. Ignoring possible limitations does not make them go away; addressing them assures your reader that you have taken them into account. If your findings show that the theories that went into your planning aren't holding true, or the methods you're using do not support your hypotheses about what will work with this population, admit it. We've said it before—there's no point in continuing a program that doesn't work, so figuring out through evaluation that you should exit NOW is just as valuable (though admittedly not as much fun) as figuring out that you've hit a home run.

Step 6: Ensuring Use and Sharing Lessons Learned

Until you share findings with stakeholders, your evaluation isn't finished. Evaluation results and recommendations should inform program improvements, help you decide whether a program should be continued or expanded (or not), and provide insight into designing future programming efforts. In some cases, you ought to "publish" your results in some form so that your colleagues in other communities can benefit from your work. Many best practices programs now exist; NACCHO has an excellent program for identifying and publicizing "model practices" at its national meeting, for instance.

Your evaluation planning should include how you will use the findings. Uses may vary. The Peer Power team used evaluation results to recommend expanding the program from one county to a region of counties. (They also published a summary of the results in the *Journal of Public Health Management and Practice.*)[2] Evaluation results of the Management Academy itself have been used to demonstrate to the initial funders that the pilot program was successful, and to show prospective new customers and partners that the program will work for them too. The important thing is that you've thought through why you are evaluating your program.

There are two principles to ensuring that you use evaluation results and recommendations. First and foremost, the audience for the evaluation findings must be clear. Second, it follows that you tailor your presentation to that audience. Is the primary audience program personnel, funders, or partners? Does this audience want a technical report, a presentation, or a brief with key recommendations?

Some evaluators and program personnel may think that a long technical report is required for all evaluations. For record keeping purposes, notes on all aspects of the evaluation are necessary, but a full technical report may not be. In fact, a technical report may backfire if it buries the recommendations with too much detail. Evaluation results can be transmitted through many forms—a full evaluation report (if needed), brief reports, in-person presentations, brochures, published articles, community forums, and more. If there are several stakeholders, several methods to transmit findings may be needed. During the design phase of the evaluation, ask stakeholders what method for communicating the results they prefer. Evaluators and program personnel need to build in sufficient time and resources for these various reporting requirements.

The Management Academy website provides evaluation results through many of the methods described here. These are helpful examples to consider as you plan your evaluation and want to ensure that it is used.[3]

Getting Professional Evaluation Assistance

There is not room here for us to teach you everything you need to know to do a thorough evaluation of your program. For example, "analyzing data" properly is a much more complex undertaking than we have space to describe here. People spend years of doctoral-level work learning the appropriate techniques for analysis and interpretation, keeping abreast of the literature so that they can put their evaluations into a comparative context with evaluations of other programs, and understanding the various methods of collecting information. Our goal in this chapter is not to make you experts in evaluation. After reading this chapter, in fact, you might decide to hire a professional evaluator to help you design and conduct your evaluation, particularly if future funding or other important decisions ride on that evaluation. Hiring professional assistance will make your job easier, and it might add credibility to your findings by providing an unassailably objective viewpoint. On the other hand, we hope that even if you can't hire a professional, our suggestions can get you started on a road that too few public health organizations take—the road toward understanding how and why their programs succeed (or don't).

It should be clear to you at this point that the time to bring in that expert is now, because at least half of the usefulness of evaluation planning comes in the design phase, before implementation.

What Can Go Wrong?

1. Your measures of success are not detailed enough.

As we said earlier, you don't have to describe your evaluation plan in great detail in your business plan. However, your business plan should indicate how you'll know that your program is working. You must spend time considering what specific measures you'll use to indicate success at providing the service or product and what measures will indicate its effect in the target population. Find evaluation resources in a book or on the Web, or consult an evaluation specialist, for generating these SMART measures.

2. You don't plan time/money for evaluation.

Make sure you include time and money specifically for evaluation and quality control when you create your timeline and your budget. If it isn't on the timeline and isn't in the budget, it isn't going to happen. Don't wait until you implement to think about how you will evaluate.

Building an Evaluation Plan

Knowing the answers to the following questions will help you plan your program, even if you don't put them into your business plan proper.
Building a logic model:

1. What **resources/inputs** (funding, partners, networks, staff, time, facilities, and policies) will go into or affect your program?

2. What **activities** (processes, techniques, tools, actions, products, services) will the program involve?

3. What **outputs** (services and products delivered or produced) do you expect?

4. What **outcomes** (specific changes in the target group) do you expect?

5. What **impacts** (organizational, community, or system level changes) do you expect?

Gathering evidence:

1. What type of information does each of your stakeholders need about your program? To what use will each put this information?

2. Using the SMART model (specific, measurable, action-oriented, realistic, and time-limited), draft three (3) questions you would like to answer about your program.

References

1. Collins, Jim. *Good to Great*. New York: HarperBusiness, 2001.
2. Thomas, Anne B., and Ellie Ward. Peer Power: How Dare County, North Carolina, is addressing chronic disease through innovative programming. *J Public Health Management Practice*. 2006;12(5):462–467.
3. See the Management Academy website at www.maph.unc.edu. Other evaluation resources include the American Evaluation Association, at www.eval.org, and the CDC Evaluation Working Group site, at http://www.cdc.gov/eval/resources.htm.

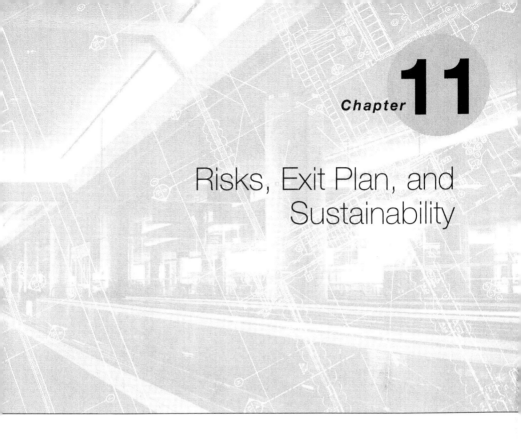

11

Risks, Exit Plan, and Sustainability

Any good plan has contingencies. An important purpose of the business planning process is to identify potential risks and try to limit their impact. Entrepreneurs and their funders want to find out what could go wrong and then decide whether or not the risks are manageable. Thus most business plans, as part of their risk analysis, include a section on the "exit plan." Airline staff always point out the emergency exits before the plane takes off, even though they are confident you won't need them. In the rare event that you do need them, you will be prepared. The exit plan section of your business plan outlines the steps for undoing a project if it doesn't work for some reason (that is, if one of the bad things you thought might be a risk actually happens). It also accounts for the intentional exit, when getting out of the program is part of your plan.

Exiting

The goal of the standard exit plan is to demonstrate that failure—no matter how unlikely—will not be catastrophic. Staff can be reassigned, space can be reallocated, financial losses can be managed, alliances with partners can be ended without damaging relationships. Your exit plan reassures your audience that your organization will survive if things don't go as planned.

These are examples of planning for *accidental* exits, but you should also imagine an *intentional* exit. Your exit plan can be very useful for this purpose. Think for a moment about how exit planning is used in the private sector. Some business plans are written with the express purpose of building a new venture that a larger company will want to acquire. The plan is explicit: launch, get big, then sell out. Selling off is an unlikely outcome of your public health plan. Much more likely is the spin-off scenario: a plan for a new venture that starts life inside a larger company, but becomes its own entity later if it is successful. The exit plan is tightly linked to the sustainability plan in this case: it lays out how the new venture will exit smoothly and then sustain itself without the support of the larger organization.

A friend of ours leads just such a spin-off company: it started inside a large regional bank as a group that provided customer resource management (CRM) services. CRM is an approach that studies existing customers to find out what additional services they might be interested in purchasing, then tries to sell those services to them. This group was useful to the bank they worked for, but over time they became even more valuable to other banks because they had developed systems and software that could work anywhere. So the CRM group was spun off and now is a stand-alone company, providing CRM data and consulting services to mid-sized banks across the country.

The same thing happens in governmental organizations. The Hot Springs School District in Arkansas some years ago wanted to know how students were doing in key learning areas—as a way to help students, teachers, and administrators understand the schools' strengths and weaknesses. The school district started a new venture to provide real-time testing results. The program, called "Learning Institute," which was launched the year before "No Child Left Behind" was instituted, was so successful that it was spun off as a private company in 2006. The company now does testing and analysis for school districts across Arkansas and has begun offering their services to other states as well.[1]

Many of the best Management Academy business plans are tightly integrated with one or more community partners, to the point that often the partners assume responsibility for the plan. Often this looks like the best possible solution to addressing public health issues. Take the issue of obesity: many in public health see sedentary lifestyles as an important contributing factor. Public health department staff are probably not best suited for opening up work-out facilities, or clearing trails, or starting jogging clubs. You are best at the organizational and policy level, helping others understand the dimensions of the problem and using groups to find sensible, effective solutions. Let someone else put in the sweat equity over the long haul.

In general, public health organizations function very well in the role of convener. At its best, your organization understands what's needed to insure the health of the public, integrates science and practical knowledge, and serves as the bridge to connect partners from different sectors and different backgrounds. In other words, you are good at starting new ventures: seeing opportunities and putting community resources together. If that's the area where you do your best work—starting new ventures—maybe you should always try to spin them off! Running programs takes time and energy away from starting new programs. The exit plan section of the business plan encourages you to plan in advance how and when you will stop doing the direct work so that you can go on to the next start-up.

Perhaps that's too optimistic. Here's the pessimistic take: public health priorities will continue to shift rapidly, making it difficult and undesirable to commit to programs long term. Make sure you plan in advance how to exit from programs in an orderly way. You won't be ready for the onslaught of future priorities unless you have a way to exit from the programs you are planning today.

Risks

Don't think about all the risks at the beginning of a project. You might get so bogged down that you never get beyond the idea. In fact, we suggest you make a rule during brainstorming that no one is permitted to talk about why an idea won't work. You can probably think of someone in your organization whose strength is imagining disastrous futures for any possible plan. They act as "barrier finders," like a stud-finder in carpentry. Barrier finders in organizations are good at letting you know what could go wrong with any project. Don't invite these people to the brainstorming session.

When it comes time for writing the risk section, however, you want to enlist your barrier finder, or at least dust off your own barrier-finder abilities. The point of the risk section is to analyze all the possible threats to the plan you've just developed so carefully (and optimistically). What if a key staff member is lost? What if reimbursement rates fall? What if the new administration changes direction? What if new priorities pull resources away? What if partners can't fulfill their obligations? What if the legal/regulatory environment changes? What if gas prices go up 50% in four months, as they did in summer 2005? What if your lease falls through? Every plan has risks that are more or less likely to happen. Knowing what they are might improve how you design your plan.

Most of you in public health have gained a rich appreciation of the benefits of crisis preparedness in the years since 2001. The exercise of imagining what could go wrong makes you better in an emergency. It also makes you feel more secure in launching a new project.

Planning for the Accidental Exit

Government organizations are generally risk-averse: decision makers will want to know the risks in some detail before launching a new project. New projects that require hiring new staff, for instance, can be difficult and expensive to shut down. So it helps to think in advance about what could happen that would require shutting down (e.g., can't find start-up funds; insufficient interest from target market; revenues don't come in as expected; partners quit), and how you would shut down if it became necessary.

Sometimes "risks" are not, in and of themselves, bad events. The state could start offering the very service you plan to provide, for example. This is good for customers, but it would mean you would need to take an accidental exit from your program. A good exit plan will be very practical and clear about what could change the project's course or make it untenable or unnecessary. It will also lay out plans for exiting that will work in many different situations, not just the ones you foresee. It has been said that, although New York's many disaster plans didn't account for terrorists using planes to destroy buildings, they did account for plane crashes, fires in high-rises, and terrorist attacks. In 2001, New York officials pieced together a crisis response from the parts of several different plans.

The following example, from a plan to provide integrated mental health services at a health department in western North Carolina, describes two situations in which the accidental exit would be necessary:

> The provision of integrated mental health services by the Buncombe County Health Center would be discontinued under two scenarios. The first would occur if the necessary fees for services could no longer be generated. This could happen if government sources decrease their reimbursement schedules and alternative funding cannot be found. The program would be closed and clients referred to any available community resources (this would be a highly undesirable option for our population).
>
> A second exit scenario could occur if a private agency were willing to provide quality on-site integrated mental health services at the Buncombe County Health Center at a reduced cost. Outsourcing of services would require credible quality assurance

oversight including monitoring of client satisfaction. The proposed program in this business plan provides essential mental health services to an economically disadvantaged population. These services are unlikely to be delivered in a cost effective manner by any other model. We anticipate that this program will need to continue indefinitely in order to address the serious burden of mental health in our community.

This assessment shows that the planners have realistically and soberly considered what might affect their program, how they would exit if necessary, and what might be the effect on customers.

Specific Risks to Consider

Our research into Management Academy team outcomes suggests a few key areas where things can go wrong and force you to make an unintentional exit from a public health business plan.

1. Lack of supervisor/organization support

The most common reason cited in our data for teams that fail to implement their plans 'is the lack of supervisor support. Your immediate boss and the bosses and stakeholders up the line have lots of influence over whether you implement or not. In general this barrier will be evident before you start to implement, but not always. Many of you in governmental public health have "many masters" to serve: county officials, city officials, district officials, state officials, and boards of various kinds, for instance. Nonprofit partners have decision makers and board oversight as well. Consider the possibility that someone in that chain could shut down the program at some point, and then plan preventive measures. Communication and involving these stakeholders in your planning are ways to help keep this barrier out of your way.

2. Lack of money

As you might have guessed, lack of money is a common reason for teams' failure to implement. The point of your learning the business plan model is to develop a new public health venture that is going to generate revenue ... eventually. Most plans need start-up funds, though, and the source of these funds is often in question. Indeed, the funds themselves may be dependent on the quality of your business plan! Your exit plan section can include an analysis of what you would do if start-up money were not available (or not available in the amount you need to launch).

Your business plan process is meant to figure the likelihood that, given a certain amount of start-up money, the program will generate revenue and become sustainable. Throughout the process, you have worked hard to make rational assumptions. But you make so many assumptions in business planning, chances are that some of the assumptions are wrong. It isn't possible to know in advance which assumptions are wrong, of course. You can, however, figure out which assumptions are the most important, in other words, which assumptions would require you to exit if they changed.

If you charge a usage fee, for instance, your revenues will be dependent on the number of users. Figure out what would happen to your budget if you don't get the users you expect. At what point would you have to exit based on insufficient usage? If you plan to get reimbursed for services, your revenues might be dependent on third-party payers. Decide in advance how and when to exit if reimbursement rules change for the worse. And plan for fluctuation. A program providing services to college students will not collect much revenue in the summer. If you've planned for that, you won't need to exit.

3. Staff, turnover, time limitations

Lack of time/lack of staff is similarly a common reason for teams' failing to implement. It is quite common for teams in our program to abandon their plans because a teammate changed jobs or changed priorities and could no longer help with implementation. Unlike lack of money—which most teams foresee as a barrier—lack of staff is not often recognized as a barrier to future plans, according to our research. Even teams that had plans fail because of staff turnover don't see staff turnover as a future barrier!

The staff barrier is sometimes related to the first two barriers: money and supervisor support go a long way toward setting staff priorities. Good groundwork in those areas—communicating your plan early and often to the boss, for instance—helps protect the staff time you need. Another important preventive measure here is succession planning. Do you have qualified managers ready to step forward if necessary? Who should be involved now in case key personnel become unavailable in the future? Another preventive measure is to involve the right people at the beginning of the project so they have buy-in and role clarity. Finally, you must think about how you will exit gracefully if key staffers can't fulfill their roles and can't be replaced.

4. Legal/policy barriers

Several teams have reported to us that they had to exit their business plans when they found legal or policy barriers during implementation. Ideally you would uncover such problems in advance, but policies and regulations can change. Also, the very uniqueness of your program might make overcoming regulatory barriers difficult. For example, one Management Academy team from Virginia designed a first-of-its-kind regional health information database and data-sharing organization, but getting nonprofit status for this new organization was more difficult than expected. Eighteen months and $80,000 later they were still responding to an IRS national office that had "never ruled on anything like this before." Think about the areas of your plan that might be susceptible to such barriers and develop contingency plans. In the case of the Virginia team, important stakeholders stepped forward with money to carry the program while it continued to pursue the 501(c)3 nonprofit designation.

5. Other resource needs

Depending on your plan, other resources besides money and staff time might play key roles in your success or failure. Plans with transportation components might rely on vehicles, appropriately licensed drivers, fuel. Many plans require space. Perhaps you are planning a program with the school system: what if enrollments grow and the school can't afford to give you a room any more? Bricks-and-mortar projects often require land. Many public health programs rely on community support. Think carefully about the resource needs of your plan and what might happen to put pressure on those resources.

The exit plan section should prepare you to deal with specific threats that look most likely to cause failure, and also lay out general strategies for shutting down in case something unforeseen happens. So your exit plan should be linked to specific risks that you think are the most likely—with specific plans for how to exit in those cases—and should also be useful to the person managing the program as a template for shutting down in other cases.

Planning the Intentional Exit

We've been talking about assessing risks and planning for an unintentional exit. Let's turn now to the next degree of difficulty: the intentional exit.

To fully appreciate the uses of the exit plan for intentional exits, let's back up and first review principles. Your goal as a public health leader is to create the conditions under which people in your area of influence can be healthy. A blue-ribbon panel at the Institute of Medicine outlined three principal functions of public health agencies: *assessment, assurance, and policy development. Assessment* is clear: in this book we've talked extensively about assessing the needs of a specific target market group, for instance. Assessing health is a key strength for public health organizations. *Policy development*, which is beyond the scope of this book, is a powerful tool for creating conditions under which people can be healthy. That leaves assurance. *Assurance* says that, whatever people need in order to be healthy, you will ensure that they get it. You may not always provide the service, but you will make sure the service is provided by someone.

"Making sure a service is provided" is the best use of the intentional exit plan. It encourages you to think into the future of your project, to a time when your organization is no longer running it. Assume that you will not be running this program forever. If not you, who? Are they ready to take over now? What would make them ready? How will the transition happen? These are the questions the exit plan encourages you to answer.

Playing to Your Strengths

What is your organization great at? Public health organizations aren't all the same, but many are great at assessment: assessing health needs and finding root causes. These strengths make it possible for you to design efficient solutions that prevent problems before they get expensive and dangerous. This model applies to many different areas of public health: finding and responding to outbreaks, preparing for hazards, educating people about health issues, developing partnerships, crafting policies.

Being great at assessment and analysis is a big job—and being great at these things means trying to limit the amount of time you spend on other things (at which you are less great and in which you are less interested). That's one reason that so many grant-funded programs in public health end when the grants end: more assessment work looms, and you are on to the next priority need. Public health agencies typically have flat or declining budgets; you can't afford the resources (time and money) to continue every program you start.

You do not want programs to fail, of course, and neither do the initial funders of those programs. Neither do the community constituents. You want what is typically called "sustainability." Funders want programs to sustain themselves, because sustainability increases their amount of mission-fulfillment per dollar. Communities want programs to sustain themselves—assuming that they get value from the program. Public Health officials want programs to sustain themselves—assuming the program creates public health value, and assuming the effort doesn't have to come entirely from the public health department.

Hence the business plan that creates a road map to a sustainable revenue-generating program, hence the exit plan that creates a road map to transitioning a program smoothly to partners who are willing and able to sustain the effort.

A review of some successful Management Academy business plans will show what is meant about sustainability and partnership. Here is a short list of business plans submitted since spring 2000 that have been successfully implemented. All were started up with significant input from governmental public health, but were implemented and/or sustained with community partners in the lead role.

A Mother's House is a program that provides interim housing to high-risk pregnant women, primarily from high-poverty areas of southeast Georgia, who would otherwise have been admitted to the hospital. The program was part of a broad public health initiative in southeast Georgia to decrease pre-term delivery and improve birth outcomes. This plan was carried forward by the regional hospital, which had both public health and financial incentives to keep it going. The program placed the women in a comfortable dormitory-like setting with nursing support, close to the hospital in Savannah. Taking these high-risk patients out of inpatient beds made the patient's stay easier and saved millions in Medicaid dollars.

Peer Power is a program that trains high school students to teach middle school students about healthy eating, physical activity, and other healthy living choices. Peer Power was launched in July 2001; it was a fully integrated part of the core health education curriculum in Dare County's three middle schools beginning with the 2002-2003 school year and continuing since then. The positive relationship that existed between administration of the Dare County Department of Public Health and the Dare County Schools allowed the strategic partnership to prosper with minimal effort and secured the requisite buy-in for this initiative to occur within the schools.

Electronic Medical Records: In the "lakelands" district of South Carolina, on the rural western border of the state, the Lakelands Rural Health Network (LRHN) was formed to provide local primary care providers with a comprehensive electronic records system. Seven partner organizations who represented key players in the area health care system, and the "safety net" for residents of this part of South Carolina, came together to create the plan. A HRSA Network Development grant offset some of the initial project costs, and the remaining initial and ongoing costs are managed though provider fees charged to participating primary care practices. LRHN functions as the administrator of the project, contracting with the technology provider for the needed software, training, and technology services on behalf of the participating providers, who contract to pay for the service.

What This Means

In each of these cases, the business plan implementations were successful in part because the plans made rational assumptions about where effort would be available over several years. Generally, these plans assumed that governmental public health staff would be more involved at the beginning phases of assessment and planning and implementing, and less involved in longer-term execution and sustainability. Their business plan reflected this assumption.

The exit plan is a critically important section for public health business planning. Your organizations are risk-averse: this section helps show that the risks are known and manageable. Your organizations are great at assessment, program development, and partnering: this section helps plan how to spin off a program as a way of increasing the chances of long-term sustainability.

What Can Go Wrong?

Avoid some of the following pitfalls we've seen in Management Academy teams, and you'll go a long way toward building sustainability into your program:

1. Business plan is too optimistic

The plan avoids naming some fairly obvious risks or downplays risks too much. Naming the risks—especially if they are significant—demonstrates that you have done your analysis well. If you can name it, you can tame it.

2. Fails to adjust plan to deal with assessed risk

This is the plan that lists potential risks but doesn't show how to manage them. The plan becomes more of a narrative than a real business plan. A narrative typically runs chronologically from beginning to end. In contrast, the different sections of your business plan should respond to and support each other.

3. Neglects to consider an intentional exit

Exit plan only deals with unintentional exits and misses the opportunity to plan for transfer of effort in the future.

Plan to Keep on Planning

You can very well assume that virtually everything you base your plan on will change. The constant is the planning itself: keep planning, and you will find that the process gets easier and the product better. Many teams that attend the Management Academy must postpone or abandon the plans they write for the Academy. A survey of graduates from the most recent years found that 65% had done so. But half of the group that postponed one plan had implemented other revenue-generating projects instead. In other words, it's the planning, rather than the product, that is ultimately more important. For one thing, once you have written a public health business plan and launched a program, you'll find yourself thinking differently about new challenges that come your way.

Building Your Risks and Exit Plan Section

1. List at least five (5) things that, if they happen, could cause you to abandon your plan (ordered by likelihood).

2. For each of the risks you've listed, list a strategy for responding to it.

3. If you have to unintentionally exit, what will be required to shut down the program? Consider especially space, materials and equipment, staff, stakeholder communications, and money. What would be the costs associated with shutting down? Who will bear them?

4. If the program becomes a sustainable model, what organization is best positioned to run it long term? Outline the steps necessary to transfer operations to that organization.

References

1. See their website, www.thelearninginstitute.net, for more information about the Learning Institute.

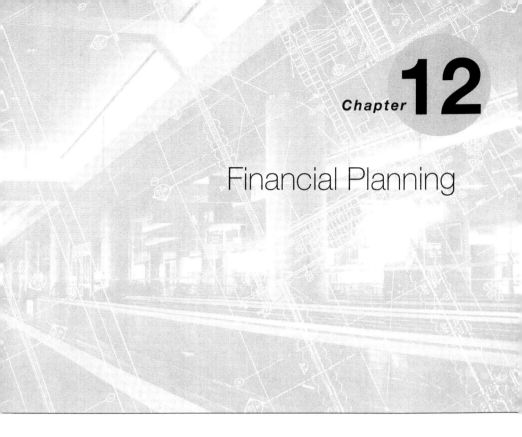

Chapter 12

Financial Planning

A s we've said before, our Management Academy for Public Health is a joint program of the UNC School of Public Health and the Kenan-Flagler Business School. Our teachers of financial planning are professors from Kenan-Flagler, and they cover much more than writing business plans in their classes. We include here what we believe you need to know to analyze and present financial assumptions in your business plan.

Financial Sustainability

As important and unique as your proposed program is, all programs have one thing in common: they need start-up money to be implemented and a continuing source of money to be sustained. Many important programs fail, not because they don't fill a need, but because they run out of funding. Programs that rely solely on grants or government support (local, state, or federal) are dependent on those funding sources being renewed year after year to continue operations. When the priorities of the funding organization change, your program could lose its funding.

Your business plan is designed to help prevent that from happening. It should be, in effect, a template for creating a hard-to-kill program. If you have been around public health for very long, you have had the chance to see how and why good programs end. Think about the last few rounds of budget cuts in your state or agency: what programs were vulnerable? Different dimensions of a program would be reviewed in determining which programs to cut—but certainly the fiscal dimension is central. Three conditions in particular make it easy for decision makers to cut programs:

1. Generate no revenue

If your organization is facing a cut in its budget, it doesn't make sense to cut programs that bring money in (especially if their revenues help cover overhead costs for the organization). Instead you would cut programs that send money out.

2. Use resources inefficiently

It is easy to cut programs that, relative to other programs, get fewer results per dollar spent. To guarantee sustainability, make sure your program is getting good results across a broad number of groups/people, in an efficient manner.

3. Have a big budget in a low-priority area

The issue here is the cost (in money, time, people, reputation) versus importance. Cutting big-budget programs in general is tempting, if that big budget can be shifted to fund several small-budget programs you want to save. Cutting big-budget programs is even easier if it seems that no one in the community will complain much. You can control this by aligning what you attempt to do with the highest priorities of your organization.

The business planning discipline encourages you to build programs that are important, efficient with resources, get good outcomes, and create their own revenue. These are the programs that avoid the scrap heap when money gets tight. The money issue is just one of the decision points, but it is critically important. Revenue by itself is a protective factor, of course, but money is part of the "efficiency" dimension as well (because efficiency is basically outcomes per dollar). In fact, in our economic system, a program's ability to generate revenue is often viewed as one indication that it is in fact important.

So the finance section is critically important if you want to build a sustainable program that won't get cut in tough fiscal times. The finance section of your business plan is similar to other program plans or grant proposals you have written in many respects. The finance section requires you to think through the financial needs for starting your program, and then forecast all the costs and expenses of operating it. Unlike most grant proposals, it requires you to show also how you will create the revenue to pay for those expenses in the long term.

Revenue Generation

Successful public health business plans have a significant source of revenue generation built into the plan. Generating revenue means freedom from the annual scramble for continuing grant funds, and freedom from the impact of waning political interest or tax revenue shortfalls.

Your program can generate revenue by selling a product, or charging a fee for a service you provide, or through strategic alliances with other organizations in the public and private sectors. Keep in mind that the person or entity receiving the service or product does not necessarily have to be the person or entity paying you the fees or purchasing the product. For example, a service fee for providing a dental exam to a patient may be paid by a private insurance company or by Medicaid or Medicare. If the patient pays, you could institute a sliding scale based on the patient's income or resources. The fee for a participant in a weight loss class might be covered by an employer, a church, or directly by the participant. One way to think imaginatively about revenue generation is to ask who stands to benefit from your program. A healthy community member is a benefit to the community. Hospitals benefit from good preventive care that keeps people from visiting an emergency room for diabetes complications. Employers benefit from workers who have access to after-hours primary care or other services. Schools benefit from having children inoculated against the flu. Ask who benefits, and you may come up with creative ways to generate revenue that do not involve charging a fee to the recipient of the program.

Grants can be invaluable as start-up funding sources, but history suggests that they are not reliable long-term funding sources. Most organizations that fund programs through grants prefer to see that the grantee has a sustainability plan to continue the program once the grant funds have been depleted. So, developing integrated revenue generation in your business plan will serve two purposes: it will make your program more competitive to potential granting organizations for start-up funding, and it will allow program effort to continue in the long term without relying too much on outside sources for funding.

Revenue versus Profit

Many public health managers are taken aback by the idea of generating revenue. "But we are here to provide a service," they say, "not make a profit!" Here it is important to understand the distinction between *revenue* and *profit*. *Revenue* is money an organization receives for its activities, often in exchange for a product or service. This is what the organization uses to pay its expenses. In addition to writing grants, government and nonprofit organizations generate revenue by charging for things: water, site inspections, preventive care, neighborhood environmental screenings, computer training, or educational presentations. *Profit*, on the other hand, is the amount of revenue left over after all expenses have been paid—if any.

All organizations must find some way to pay their expenses. Generating revenue for the activities of a program makes that program viable for the long term, rather than being dependent on the priorities of outside funding agencies or governmental budgets. Generating revenue to cover expenses for your program may actually be in the best interest of your program beneficiaries because a financially sustainable program is more likely to last for the long term than a program that relies solely on outside funding sources.

So you always need to have enough revenue to cover your expenses (wherever the revenue comes from). Turning a profit—having an excess of revenue over expenses—is optional. If you plan your budget carefully, you will cover your expenses without incurring the wrath of taxpayers by taking in more money than you spend.

Financial Assumptions

Revenue and expense values in your budget must be arrived at through assumptions. Good assumptions are based on data, not guesses. Include a narrative section in your financials outlining these assumptions, both to keep you financially on track when you implement your plan, and to help readers of your business plan—including potential funding sources—see exactly how all numbers on your operations budget were derived. To be convinced that your financial numbers are reasonably accurate, they will want to see what assumptions you have made and decide how good those assumptions are.

Consider the assumptions related to salary expense. Your operations budget will show the total you will be paying out annually in salaries. Your narrative of budget assumptions would describe your thinking about what goes into that salary total. Imagine the questions that a funder/decision maker might have: What positions will your project include? What is the total salary for each position? How much effort will be required from each position (FTE)? How did you decide on this level of effort? Is your effort assumption based on history, agency guidelines, benchmarking with other organizations, interviews with front-line staff? How is this level of effort connected to the program plan you have already described? How much will be paid in benefits, and how did you calculate that figure? What percentage annual increase is expected for each salary? Every item on your budget potentially raises questions of this sort. The goal is to think through these details and write down exactly what assumptions you have made to build your cost budget.

Note that your finance section is closely linked to the analysis you made in earlier sections. Your salary assumptions should line up with what you said in your operations section about how much staff effort you would require. Most of your revenue assumptions will be linked to the size of your target market and the percentage of that target market you expect to serve. You will need to determine the per-unit price or fee you will charge for each product or service in your plan, taking into account all the costs you will incur, and multiply that fee by how many units you expect to serve. These numbers should be clearly justified in your budget narrative section and sensibly linked to operations, target market, and other appropriate sections.

Most of all, your numbers should be realistic: don't fudge on your revenue numbers. Of course you *want* to cover your expenses and you *hope* you can cover your expenses. But what can you reasonably *expect* to earn the first year? The second year? Being unrealistic at this stage will cost you in the implementation phase. Unreasonable expectations of what you can earn will result very quickly in budget trouble. In grant-writing, unrealistic budgeting sometimes works as a strategy: the penalty for overestimating how popular your service will be is that your expense budget is easier to manage. The worst-case scenario is that next time you have to find a different funder because you missed your numbers. In business planning, unrealistic revenue budgeting ALWAYS gets punished: if the customers you predicted don't show up, the revenue doesn't show up either, and good luck covering your expenses. Most businesses expect to have a deficit in the first few years, and a realistic goal would be to cover expenses with revenues by Year 5.

Part of being realistic is outlining how you expect cost figures to increase each year and recognizing that there may be different sources of funding at different stages of your program. Grants or other start-up funds can help cover operating costs in the first couple of years. If that is your expectation, be sure not to inflate your revenue numbers—otherwise you will underestimate the amount of start-up money you need.

Your main objective in the financial assumptions section of your business plan is to walk your reader through all of the numbers in your operations budget. Use the section to clarify how you derived each of the numbers, for both revenue and expenses, what assumptions went into your decisions, and what percentage you used to calculate increases year to year. Based on this section, anyone reading your operations budget should have a clear sense of where your budget numbers came from and should be able to refer to this section to answer any questions they have when looking at your operations budget.

Operations Budget

The operations budget is a table or spreadsheet that details what it will cost to run your program and what money will come in to cover those costs. An essential component of any business plan, the operations budget is a useful tool for planning your financial needs, and often serves to set benchmarks with which to assess your financial progress along the way. It is the plan you use to make sure for yourself—and show to others—that you will have enough money to implement your program.

In structuring your operations budget, group your revenues on the top half of the page. Every source of money or in-kind resource goes on the top half. Expenses are listed underneath. Each revenue or expense should have its own line item. Reading the list of expense items on the bottom half should give readers a clear impression of exactly what you need to spend money on in order to run the program. The top half shows exactly where the money is going to come from to pay for those things. Clearly, this budget should include nothing that you haven't already talked about somewhere else in the business plan. Revenue and expense items should all look familiar to a careful reader of your plan.

You should show annual operations budgets for the first five years. This will show readers how the program revenues and expenses will change over time. In addition, you should show a monthly operations budget for the first year. Again, this monthly budget should reflect when you expect to actually incur expenses or receive revenues. Don't just divide the annual figures by twelve. The monthly budget helps show how quickly the program will start up: how much will it cost to get ready to run the program? How much time will be necessary to do things like train people, organize, develop materials, do preliminary marketing? When will revenue start flowing in? Will it flow consistently, or in spurts?

In-kind Donations

Most of the budgets we see for public health business plans include in-kind donations. In-kind donations should appear in your operations budget as a dollar amount, reflecting the value of the donation. Anything of value that will be donated—rent, utilities, salary support, supplies, advertising, whatever—should appear on your budget. Estimate the dollar value of each in-kind donation, then enter that dollar value on both the top and the bottom half: first as revenue and again as expense. The two entries will cancel each other out. Notice that your revenue related to expenses doesn't change. It shouldn't: you didn't actually bring any money in and you didn't actually pay any money out. But you did increase the value of your program, and that value is now reflected in the size of your budget.

A reader should be able to look at the budget and know immediately which expenses are covered by in-kind donations. Think of it this way: assume that your partner organization is providing space as an in-kind contribution. Rent for that space is an expense that costs $2,000 a month. In the bottom half of your operations budget, you should include an expense line for rent. In this case "Rent" is also a gift, which is to say revenue: your partner is putting $2,000 worth of space into the program. So mark the expense for rent as "In-Kind" and, in the top half of your operations budget, include a revenue line for In-Kind Rent. This method acknowledges the value of the donation to the program and allows you to see how much additional revenue you would need to earn if you had to pay for rent at some point. The result is a realistic picture of the financial footprint of your program.

Start-up Financing

Start-up financing is funding to be used for one-time expenses to get a program up and running. Start-up expenses can include things such as purchasing equipment, developing staff, or funding ongoing expenses in the first year or two, before revenue stabilizes. This funding is often from gifts, in-kind donations, or grants: one-time sources of money. Revenues for start-up should decline over time until the program is fully functional. After the start-up phase, what's left is an operational budget. In our experience, grant-makers are unlikely to contribute to operational expenses after a reasonable start-up or pilot period.

Break-even Analysis

The break-even point is the point at which your cost and revenue balance each other out. The break-even analysis is an optional addition to your financial section. Its purpose is to show at what point your revenue will cover your expenses. We do not recommend that you complete a break-even analysis if you don't ever plan to have your revenue cover all your expenses. If you do expect your program to become completely self-sustaining at some point from revenues only (with no use of in-kind donations or grants), a break-even analysis will help you determine the point at which that will happen.

Break-even analysis is useful for two reasons: first it shows the relationship between volume and price, and second it helps explain the important difference between your fixed and variable costs. Break-even does not need to happen in the first year of operations (and rarely does).

At the break-even point, you are not losing money, not relying on outside funding or in-kind support, and you are not making a profit. You have just covered the cost of operating your program—both fixed cost and variable cost. *Fixed expenses* are predictable costs such as rent, utilities, salaries, and advertising. Fixed expenses are associated with the normal course of doing business and have to be paid regardless of volume. Even if you have no customers, you have to pay the rent and the salaries. These fixed expenses are easily determined, and they usually stay at the same level regardless of your level of service provision or product sales (at a certain point they might "step up" to another level based on your volume—that would reflect that you needed to hire a new staff member or rent more space, for instance. More about that later).

You must also cover expenses that vary according to how many customers you have. *Variable expenses* are those expenses that are directly associated with the services you provide or products that you sell. Medical supplies, a screening kit, a folder of educational materials— all are examples of variable costs that your program may incur with each new customer.

With your total fixed costs and your variable cost per unit (all of the variable costs that are associated with making one product or performing service on one client), you understand your expenses. To calculate your break-even point you also need to figure out revenue. So these are the component parts for your break-even analysis:

- Total fixed costs
- Variable cost per unit
- Selling price or fee per unit

Break-even analysis will tell you how many units you need to sell at your price to cover all your costs.

Here are two ways to calculate your break-even point. Both are good: one or the other might make more sense to you. The first method calculates how much *each customer* will pay to cover variable expenses, and how much is left over to put toward fixed expenses. This method calculates what is called "contribution margin." Imagine a training program for food service and other organizations to help them prevent food-borne outbreaks. Your total annual fixed expenses include salaries, rent, utilities, telephone, advertising, communications/postage, and travel. Let's say these fixed expenses come to $60,000 per year. Your variable cost would include things like a workbook, a nametag, a pen, snacks, coffee, and lunch, for each participant. For demonstration purposes let's assume you can provide that stuff for $20 per person. If you anticipate charging $50 for each trainee, you can calculate your revenues to break even as follows:

Contribution margin = price – variable cost

$50 price – $20 variable cost = $30 contribution margin

So each participant pays $50, of which $20 covers materials and food; $30 goes toward everything else, like salaries and rent. If each participant is paying $30 toward your fixed expenses, it is easy to figure out how many participants you need: you need enough participants to pay for your $60,000 fixed expense.

$60,000 fixed expense / $30 contribution per person = 2,000 participants to break even.

Here's a second formula to calculate the same break-even number. This example starts by determining how much revenue you need to break even using the following formula:

(Fixed Costs) / (1 – (Variable cost per unit/Selling Price per unit)) = Revenue to Break Even

Let's say you are developing a program to provide influenza immunizations to adults. Again, your total annual fixed expenses include salaries, rent, utilities, telephone, advertising, communications/postage, and travel. We will use the same fixed expense as the other example: $60,000 per year. Your variable costs would include the vaccine and all the medical supplies necessary to inoculate one patient. For demonstration purposes let's leave the numbers the same: $20 in variable cost per screening. You anticipate $50 in revenue for each screening, so you can calculate your revenues to break even as follows:

$60,000 fixed / (1 – ($20 (variable) / $50 price)) = Break-even

$60,000 / (1 – 0.40) = Break-even revenue

$60,000 / 0.60 = Break-even revenue

$100,000 = Break-even revenue

If you know that break-even revenue is $100,000, you can easily determine the number of units you would need to sell in order to break even. Simply divide your break-even revenue by your selling price per unit. In this case

Break-even revenue / Selling price per unit = Number of units to break even

$100,000 / $50 = 2,000 units to break even

This program needs to perform 2,000 screenings per year in order to cover all of its costs. As soon as the program reaches a level of 2,000 flu shots per year, the program will be financially self-sustaining.

You may notice a couple of potential complications about this second example. First, you may notice that "fixed" expenses might actually go up eventually! Ask any nurse: there is a limit to how many vaccinations you can do with one nurse. At a certain volume point, you are going to have to bring in another nurse and/or find more space, thus changing your "fixed" expenses. The same is true of the training program: suppose you have a design that isn't effective for more than 75 learners per session. Beyond 75, you will incur extra costs for running a second session (another four hours of trainer time, another room). Be sure to determine whether there must be capacity "steps" for the program you are designing.

Notice that all the components of these equations have an impact on the break-even point. Finance is more than just math, more than just counting. It is about imagining what is going to happen when you operationalize your program—and then figuring out the implications of your assumptions about price, volume, and cost. The math skills are fairly easy—and almost worthless without good, specific assumptions. Making those assumptions requires a combination of realism and creativity. You have to know what things really cost and how long things really take, but you also have to be able to imagine what would happen if you cut the price in half, or imagine how to manage the workflow so that an assistant could help prep patients for the nurse, increasing capacity.

Models

A good budget narrative spells out in plain language the decisions and the calculations you made for each line item in your budget. It explains, or justifies, why you need a particular staff member for a certain number of hours a week; it explains how you did the math to figure out, for example, what the service would cost in salary (wage plus benefits times hours). It may explain what research you did to make key budget assumptions, or specify the types of procedures you will offer and how much they will cost. The following example is from a plan for a program providing dental health to rural North Carolinians:

> Our number of appointments in a calendar year is based on a four day/week clinic schedule, operating 48 weeks/year, with an average of 10 appointments/day for an average of 2,000 available appointments per year. A 10% no show rate is also factored in, giving us our projected kept appointments per year at 1,800.
>
> Based on research into similar programs' offerings, we estimate that about 65% of patients will receive a comprehensive oral exam,

bitewing × 2 x-ray, and a cleaning with fluoride treatment. Another 10% will receive a comprehensive oral exam, cleaning, and separate fluoride treatment. Approximately 25% of patients will receive some type of restorative treatment. Approximately 50% of patients will also require sealants on an average of 4 teeth per patient.

Table 12-1			
Projected Annual Revenue by Payment Rate and Type			
Type of Service	Payment Rate*	Total Appointments	Revenue
Exam/bitewing × 2/Prophy w/Fluoride Appts)	$96.00	1170 (65% of Appts)	$112,320.00
Exam/Prophy/Separate Fluoride	$83.00	180 (10% of Appts)	$14,940.00
Sealants × 4 ($32/tooth)	$128.00	900 (50% of Appts)	$115,200.00
Treatment	$120.00	450 (25% of Appts)	$54,000.00
Total Revenue			$296,460.00

*Payment rate based on Medicaid Reimbursement Rates for Health Departments

This plan goes on to detail the project mix of payors and payment rates for the procedures they plan to provide. They end up with a very clear table of projected revenue, as shown in Table 12-1.

The plan also details assumptions of staff needs for this volume and type of service, planned salary increases, and assumed increases in Medicaid reimbursement rates.

As you know, operations budgets have revenue at the top, expenses at the bottom. The math that created the dollar amount for each line item is explained in the budget narrative. The following example is from a business plan developed in 2003 to create a regional network of physicians and hospitals to provide free medical care and ancillary services (i.e., x-ray, lab) to uninsured workers at or below 300% poverty level. Workers and their employers pay a flat fee to be a part of the program, which provides health care services at no further cost. Case managers track services through a software program designed to establish income guidelines for uninsured workers, determine registration fees in accordance with workers' income, distribute patients among volunteering physicians, track patient compliance, report the dollar value of services, and evaluate satisfaction of physicians and clients.

We chose this budget as a good example for several reasons. First, it utilizes grant funds for start-up only: no income comes from grant funding after the first year. Second, in-kind funding decreases each year. In the fifth year of the budget, the only in-kind remaining is for space. From a business perspective, we would prefer that they eliminate all in-kind from the budget by Year 5, and the budget does

Table 12-2

Cumberland Access Project Five-Year Profit Projection

	2003		2004		2005		2006		2007	
Revenues	Amount	%	Amount	%	Amount	%	Amount	%	Amount	%
Fees	$21,600	11	$81,000	84	$164,000	88	$220,000	92	$250,000	96
Grant	$150,000	79	$0	0	$0	0	$0	0	$0	0
In Kind	$18,460	10	$15,190	16	$21,330	12	$19,070	8	$10,800	4
Total Revenues	$190,060	100	$96,190	100	$185,330	100	$239,070	100	$260,800	100
Expenses	Amount	%	Amount	%	Amount	%	Amount	%	Amount	%
Case Mgr. #1	$30,000	20	$37,080	32	$38,190	20	$39,340	16	$40,520	16
Case Mgr. #2	$0	0	$15,000	13	$30,900	16	$31,830	13	$32,780	13
Case Mgr. #3	$0	0	$0	0	$15,000	8	$30,900	13	$31,830	113
Case Mgr. #4	$0	0	$0	0	$15,000	8	$30,900	13	$31,830	13
Clerk	$15,000	10	$18,540	16	$19,100	10	$19,670	8	$20,260	8
Fringe Benefits	$11,700	8	$18,360	16	$30,730	16	$39,690	16	$40,880	17
Contract -MD	$7,560*	5	$7,790*	7	$8,030*	4	$8,270*	3	$8,530	3
Travel/Mileage	$2,925	2	$4,290	3	$7,800	4	$11,700	5	$11,700	5
Telephone	$2,500	2	$2,500	2	$2,800	1	$3,200	1	$3,500	1
Supplies	$1,750	1	$1,550	1	$2,640	1	$3,330	1	$3,500	1
Space	$5,400*	4	$5,400*	5	$10,800*	6	$10,800*	5	$10,800*	5
Marketing/Post	$2,400	2	$3,500	3	$5,500	3	$4,500	2	$4,500	2
Computer Sw	$62,000	42	$0	0	$0	0	$0	0	$0	0
Computer Hw	$2,000*	1	$2,000*	1	$2,000	1	$6,000	3	$4,000	2
Print/Copy	$1,000*	1	$1,000	1	$1,500	1	$1,500	1	$2,000	1
Furniture	$2,500*	2	$0	0	$2,500*	1	$0	0	$0	
Total Expenses	$146,735	100	$117,010	100	$192,490	100	$241,630	100	$246,630	100
Net Profit (Loss)	$43,325		(20,820)		(7,160)		($2,560)		$14,170	

*In Kind

have enough revenue to cover the cost of the space. However, this team made a political decision to continue to use the in-kind space, so they left it as in-kind in their budget. Third, none of the expenses stay flat from year to year—they have taken into account that prices rise, a seemingly obvious but often overlooked fact of the economic climate.

This team also does a good job of outlining the assumptions that helped them develop their revenue numbers:

Revenue. We have applied to the Virginia Health Care Foundation for a start-up grant of $150,000. Carry-forward funds from the start-up grant will cover losses in years 2004, 2005, and 2006. In-kind revenue includes:

- services of the Medical Director from 2003 to 2006. The CAP Medical Director is Director of the Cumberland Plateau Health District.

- space donated by the Russell County Health Department from 2003 to 2007 and Clinch Valley Community Action from 2005 to 2007
- computer hardware donated by the Southwest Virginia GMEC in 2003 and the Cumberland Plateau Health District in 2004
- printing/copying donated by the Russell County Health Department in 2003, and
- furniture donated by local businesses in 2003 and 2005.

Expenses. Cumberland Access Project (CAP) will employ 0.83 FTE case managers in 2003, 1.5 FTE case managers in 2004, 3.0 FTE case managers in 2005, and 4.0 FTE case managers in 2006 through 2007. We will employ 0.83 clerks in 2003 and 1.0 FTE clerks thereafter. Cumberland Plateau Health District will donate Medical Director services to CAP from 2003 through 2006. CAP will reimburse Cumberland Plateau for Medical Director services in 2007 and thereafter. Space costs, computer hardware, printing/copying services, and furniture will be donated as indicated in the revenue notes above. These are in-kind expenses. We will contract with a software firm to design a system that meets program requirements. The software expense listed above is the amount actually paid for customized software by an organization similar to CAP.

The sliding scale will be used to determine how much each client will be charged for registration. The sliding scale is based on the federal poverty guidelines published annually by the U.S. Department of Health and Human Services.

The section goes on to provide details of the sliding fee scale, projected enrollment, and breakdown of revenue from registration fees for the first five years of the program.

This example has room for improvement, as well. We would like to see the same level of detail for the assumptions behind the expense numbers as there is for the revenue numbers. Explain what assumptions are behind the numbers for each budget category. This team did this to a certain extent for the salaries, but should also include what the annual salary is for the position, and should explain what percentage increase is used from year to year. What percentage of salary is used to calculate fringe? Other expense categories need this level of detail as well. How is the contracted Medical Doctor's pay rate determined? What rate did they use to calculate mileage, and how many miles are they budgeting for? Where will they be driving? Where did they get their numbers for telephone, supplies, and marketing, and what rate of increase are they budgeting for each? Why does telephone stay the same in Years 1–2 and then increase each year after that? How did they determine the rate for the in-kind space, and why does that number stay flat, with the exception of doubling in Year 3? Why will they increase their space in Year 3? Why is there a computer software expense only in Year 1? Presumably, this is only for the custom software that they are having developed. They will need to purchase other computer software for other functions on the computer and will need to budget for regular software upgrades as well. And what are their assumptions for computer hardware? What about printing and copying? Why do these numbers go up only every two years rather than every year? How are they valuing the furniture that will be donated? Every number in this budget was developed using assumptions, and the narrative must indicate what these assumptions were.

Find someone to read your budget with this level of scrutiny and force you to describe your own assumptions.

One major risk with this budget is that, although it only uses grant funding for start-up, planners are relying on one grant to supply 79% of the funding in the first year. So, if they are not awarded the grant, they will not be able to get the project off the ground. We suggest that you diversify start-up funding, unless the funding has already been assured.

Finally, a note on illustrating in-kind in the budget: the way it is done here is fine, because it shows the total in-kind as revenue, and then uses asterisks to indicate where the in-kind is as expenses. Another way to do this would be to break out the in-kind expenses into a separate section of the expense part of the budget, which makes it easier to distinguish between what is in-kind and what would be paid directly.

What Can Go Wrong?

In our experience several things can go wrong with your finance section. These are the major pitfalls we've seen:

1. Section is too general, not sufficiently detailed and clear

This is a problem common to many sections, but public health planners often struggle with it in this section in particular. The best business plans have well-developed sections on operations: a good operations section will help you to forecast expenses accurately. Use the specifics of the operation to tell you where and how to make predictions about monthly expenses for the first year. Be specific: don't simply divide annual expenses by 12. Your flu program is not going to run in the summer, for instance. Being specific and accurate gets much easier if you have historical data for similar programs (either your own or someone else's).

Overly general finance assumptions cause trouble for the manager who ultimately has to implement the plan. Many such plans never get implemented because decision makers don't trust them. But some do get implemented. Think about that future manager as you write your plan (after all, the manager who implements the plan might be you).

If first-time readers have many questions about how you got your numbers, it indicates that this section is too general. Causes of an overly general finance section are many, but they include the following: "I thought that was clear," "we haven't decided how much to charge," "the business manager gave us this number and we don't know where it came from," and "we calculated an average cost based on five different kinds of service for eight different kinds of payers over the last ten years."

2. Section is too speculative

As should be clear by now, one bad assumption, even a small one, can get multiplied. A small mistake in figuring your variable cost, multiplied by several thousand units, equals a big mistake. Assumptions should be more solid and evidence-based than just guesses. Good assumptions might require you to vet your plan with front-line staff and managers, to call suppliers, to get commitments in writing from partners, to collect benchmark data by calling people who run similar programs. If two people did a calculation on a napkin at lunch, the number might be too speculative. If four people independently came up with roughly the same number using historical data, it is probably good.

Sometimes you will be wrong. We have many teams who project expenses to stay flat in areas that actually increase in cost. Insurance rates and fuel costs are two common examples of blind spots—and both can have huge effects on program costs, depending on your plan.

3. "In-kind" confused with "free"

In organizations without open budget and finance processes, it is common for managers to think that in-kind resources are free. They aren't free, even if you aren't paying cash for them. If you use resources that the organization has already paid for—space in the building, for instance—you are taking advantage of a "sunk cost." Clearly it is a good thing for you to get some benefit out of that resource—but it isn't free just because someone else paid for it. To show the real cost of your program, you need to include that in-kind resource on your operations budget. Decision makers appreciate programs that use resources efficiently. They love programs that actually contribute to paying for sunk costs. So go ahead and list those in-kind resources.

4. Not accounting for all expenses

Every expense mentioned in your operations section should be mentioned here, with a specific dollar amount attached. Many, many plans we see lose sight not only of in-kind expenses but other expenses essential for operationalizing their programs. Do you have far-flung partnerships that will involve travel to meetings and other communications costs? Are you forgetting about your electric bill? What about the specialist you will need to launch your website?

Furthermore, as you plan for the future, you should recognize that these expenses will go up and account for it. Think of the team project in 2002 that assumed health benefits costs for employees would stay the same for the next five years.

5. Little or no revenue built in

Some programs you plan will include little or no revenue. Maybe they are required by statute, or perhaps taxpayers expect them to be free for some historical reason. Still, a plan without revenue isn't a business plan. A formal business plan may be the wrong tool for the job if a program is primarily supported by grants or tax revenue. Some programs are just not very big. It is probably not worth the time and effort to write a formal business plan for a tiny program that one person runs part-time on a few thousand dollars in revenue.

6. Fear and loathing

A huge problem of finance sections of public health business plans is the fact that so many public health managers are scared of numbers, especially those preceded by dollar signs.

Since the year 2000, we have systematically asked managers seven questions about their confidence in their ability to perform basic finance tasks (like budgeting, making financial assumptions, and calculating break-even). On a scale that runs from 7 (no confidence) to 49 (high confidence), the middle-point in our groups is often in the low teens, with the largest group at 7.

Lack of confidence in this case seems to result not from a history of failure; instead it results from a lack of training and a lack of practice. It certainly isn't that these managers can't do math; they can. They simply don't know the terminology, they didn't take a finance class in college (or in their master's program), and they aren't required to know the budgets of the programs they run. They are scared of the unknown.

Finance is not simply math. It is part math (fairly straightforward math at that), and part reality: street-smarts. It isn't hard to learn the math part. The street-smarts part you get by working in the real world. In fact it may be easier to learn finance as an adult than as a college student because making good assumptions is as much about experience as anything else.

Do It Anyway

In spite of these common challenges, public health managers create business plans every day, and—more important, of course—they implement those plans and find that their financial planning was sound. And, as with anything, what doesn't work will only make your next attempt that much stronger.

Building Your Financials Section

Revenues

1. How much will you charge per unit for your product or service?

2. How many units will you sell the first year?

3. By what percentage will your sales increase each year?

4. Will you use a sliding scale for payment?

5. Will all payments be made by the client, or through a third party (such as Medicaid or private insurance)?

6. Will you use any grant funding for start-up? How much? From which funding sources? In which year(s)?

7. Will you use any in-kind? For what expenses? What will be the value of these expenses? Will you be able to decrease your in-kind support so that you are paying for these expenses with revenue?

8. Will you have any additional revenue streams?

Expenses

1. What salaries will need to be included for this program?

2. What are the FTE and annual salary for each position?

3. What are the % fringe/benefits for each position?

4. What percentage increase is used from year to year for salaries?

5. Will you need to purchase any equipment for your program? How often will you need to buy new equipment or upgrade? Will this be a regular purchase or a one-time purchase for start-up?

6. Will you need to subcontract any services (such as labs)? How much will that cost?

7. By what percentage will this expense increase each year?

8. For travel expense, what rate do you use to calculate mileage?

9. How many miles are you budgeting for?

10. Where will they be driving?/What purpose?

11. Will there be any travel expense other than mileage?

12. How much will you budget for telephone and communications?

13. By what percentage will this expense increase each year?

14. How much will you budget for supplies?

15. By what percentage will this expense increase each year?

16. How much will you budget for marketing?

17. By what percentage will this expense increase each year?

18. How much will you need to spend on space (or if in-kind, what is the market value of your space)?

19. By what percentage will this expense increase each year?

20. Will you need to increase the size of your space at any point during the program?

21. How much will you spend on overhead (if not included in the space budget)?

22. By what percentage will this expense increase each year?

23. What will you spend on training each year?

24. By what percentage will this expense increase each year?

25. What will your computer hardware and software needs be? How often will you upgrade each, and how much will it cost to upgrade?

26. Will you have a website? What will be the cost to develop, host, and manage it?

27. What will you budget for printing and copying?

28. By what percentage will this expense increase each year?

29. Will you need to pay legal fees or for an annual audit (if your organization is a 501(c)3? How much will this cost?

30. By what percentage will this expense increase each year?

31. Will you need insurance for your program? How much will it cost?

32. By what percentage will this expense increase each year?

33. What other expenses will you need to include each year?

34. By what percentage will each expense increase each year?

Chapter 13

The Feasibility Plan

Y ou've done a lot of work, read a lot of pages, and you want to start writing your business plan—so you can sell the plan, get some money, and get *doing*. Sorry—there's one more thing you should do before all that. You will want to write a feasibility plan.

A feasibility plan does two things. First, it is a place where you can explore *why* you want to implement your idea. The lion's share of the business plan will be about *how* to do it in great detail. This different orientation is reflected in the order and content of the feasibility plan's sections. We give the following feasibility plan outline to Management Academy students:

1. Short Narrative Description
2. Demonstration of Need and Target Market
3. Definition of Plan
4. Industry Analysis
5. Measurement
6. Partners/Competitors
7. Timeline
8. Financial Resources

See how you don't get to your definition of plan until *after* the demonstration of need and target market? Here, need comes first. "Measurement" here means the health goals you hope to achieve and your plan for data collection that will show progress toward those goals. The feasibility plan is partly to establish that an idea is worthy: that it meets an important need.

Second, the feasibility plan asks "should we go to the trouble of writing a business plan?" In other words, can your good idea become a sustainable program? Does the plan basically make sense, are your partners interested, and is it financially sustainable? Feasibility has different components for different ventures, but the central question is this: could this idea actually work? Or are there problems that would make it too difficult?

In the chapters preceding this one, we have already discussed the key elements that go into your feasibility plan. You might imagine the feasibility plan as an outline, or a rough draft, of the full business plan. This is the main reason we put this chapter here, instead of at the beginning of the book. We imagine that at this point, you understand the function and the elements of the business plan: now you are ready to start writing. And the writing starts with an outline—the feasibility plan—that with additional work expands into the business plan.

Writing a full business plan is quite a lot of work. Before investing months of your time and sweating out the research and writing, you would want to confirm that key stakeholders agree that the idea has potential—it is a sound approach that fills a need, fits the strategic plan, fits your assets, conforms to rules and regulations. You would want to get a rough idea about scope: how big is the target market really? You would want to confirm that your proposed partners are interested in helping. These inputs and others would help you assess financial sustainability: roughly how much would this approach cost, and is it feasible to cover those costs with revenues? The answers to these questions are the domain of the feasibility plan.

Putting your feasibility plan on paper will save time. It saves you some time later if the answer is "yes, the idea is feasible," because you will use big chunks of the feasibility plan when you go on to write your formal business plan. Putting your feasibility plan on paper saves you even more time later if you decide the idea is not feasible. In our experience, several teams each year find out in the course of feasibility planning that the answer to the feasibility question is "no." We don't formally keep track, but 25% is a rough estimate. "No" might take a variety of forms for these teams: "not now," "not here," "not this way," "not with those partners," "not until the next election," "not yet." For some it takes the form of "never." As bad as some of these answers sound, any of those answers should be taken as a blessing if they save you time and help you direct your energy to the right next steps.

You might think, "If three out of four feasibility plans don't find any problems, maybe I can skip the feasibility plan!" It's true—three out of four find no problems—but in our experience, about half of those "feasible" plans actually do have problems. They just didn't get discovered initially. Every year we have teams that discover—after the feasibility plan is finished but before the business plan is finished—that something is wrong. The idea isn't feasible after all; the feasibility plan for one reason or another didn't find that out. There is no point in working to convince yourself of a plan that is ill-conceived. Better to discover now if in fact the plan is unlikely to work.

Because a good feasibility plan is a rough cut of almost everything that will go into your business plan, we won't say much more about it here. The key difference is the level of detail and the scope, as well as the focus on *why* and *whether* rather than *how*, *exactly*. In the Management Academy, teams spend about six weeks generating a feasibility plan of roughly five or six pages. In comparison, they spend six months or more generating multiple drafts of a business plan of roughly twenty pages (not including appendix material).[1]

Who Is the Feasibility Plan For?

The feasibility plan is for you and your constituents. When you've completed a good feasibility plan, you'll know whether to go on to the next idea, tweak and reassess, or go forward with a business plan. Your constituents—maybe your advisory board, or potential community partners—will know whether to give you a thumbs up or a thumbs down on this idea. Going forward means providing more details, expanding on your answers to the questions posed in the feasibility plan, and laying out a quite specific pathway for implementation—with the fairly firm knowledge that the idea can work.

What Can Go Wrong?

1. Your love for the idea blinds you to its faults

When assessing the feasibility of an idea, your role is judge, not creative artist. The creative artist plays the lead role in generating great ideas. You did that already. The feasibility planning process is supposed to figure out whether the idea has a real chance. If you advocate too hard at this point (it is your idea! you love it!), you won't find problems, and finding problems is the goal. The worst case here is to miss the potential problems and run down a dead-end road.

2. You decide to quit because it isn't feasible after all

A "no" answer is not a disaster. View it is a precursor to success. Finding problems is your goal! You succeeded! Unless you quit. Use your "no" answer to improve your chances for success later—with this idea or with a different one. There are different shades of "no" if you understand the "why." Sometimes "no" means "keep trying, it's close." Sometimes in means, "save your energy—working on a new idea will be more fruitful." Both answers help you.

What Next?

We hope you find out through this process that you can start making your public health dreams come true. Before you start, though, take a moment to check out Chapter 14, which tells the story of a Management Academy team that took their business plan all the way to implementation. It's not a typical team—but we don't come across a lot of "typical" teams. They just had a great idea—just like you.

References

1.   For a detailed description of a feasibility plan, see Orton, SN, and Anne Menkens, Business planning for public health from the North Carolina Institute for Public Health. *Journal of Public Health Management and Practice.* 2006; 12(5):489–492.

Chapter 14

Sustaining Success in South Carolina: One Team's Experience

In 2005, a team came to the Management Academy with the goal of providing comprehensive primary and preventive health care to the citizens of Florence, South Carolina. This is their story.

The team was made up of two state public health managers from the South Carolina Department of Health and Environmental Control (DHEC), and two managers from a nonprofit HIV health clinic. The clinic, called HopeHealth, provides health and other services for HIV-positive people in the city of Florence.

When the team came to the Management Academy, HopeHealth was not able to serve non-HIV+ customers because of the clinic's funding model. The goal of the team was to expand services to all who needed it, regardless of HIV status and ability to pay. The team figured that expanding service to the whole community would not only make the community healthier, it would also further their original mission by strengthening the support system for their HIV+ patients. The change would also help diversify HopeHealth's funding. This idea was the germ of what became the team's business plan.

Drawing on the skills and perspectives they learned in the Management Academy, the team created a plan for HopeHealth to become a federally recognized community health center (CHC). This designation would allow them to expand access to quality care in the city by providing a grant from HRSA and by generating fee-for-service revenue.

The plan clearly met the criteria for the Management Academy program: it drew upon a good, solid partnership; it was ambitious but seemed to be feasible; it involved revenue generation; and it fit very well with the strategic goals of the organizations involved.

The Definition of Plan

The team's plan, then, was to take what was a nonprofit health services organization that provided medical care, prevention, and support services to persons living with HIV/AIDS, and make that clinic available for all citizens of inner-city Florence. The clinic would then offer the full range of preventive, enabling, and supplemental health care services, including oral health care, mental health care, and substance abuse services, either on-site or through established arrangements with other providers, regardless of ability to pay. They would use the inner city's designation as a medically underserved area (MUA) to apply to become a community health center (CHC) and obtain "new access point" funding from the federal government, as well as special Medicaid billing rates that would provide revenue for services.

In their definition of plan, the team laid out this product service description and customer/geographic focus (inner city Florence is 98% African American) and outlined the characteristics of their clinic that would help them address this population's access, health, and social needs:

- Medical providers' scope of practice is not limited by age, sex, organ system, or disease entity. Pediatric nurse practitioner is also available.
- Specialty care and dental care is available via contracts or referral agreements with quality providers.
- Mental health and substance abuse treatment is available on-site and via contracts/referral agreements with quality providers.
- Pharmaceutical assistance will be provided (already have a 340-B pricing program).
- Counseling will be provided by a licensed master-level social worker.
- Case managers will provide basic psychosocial intervention and help clients make effective use of available resources in the community.

- Transportation will be available for all who need it.
- An outreach specialist will build rapport with persons needing to enter care and also reengage persons who may have dropped out of care.
- The culturally competent staff will treat all clients with dignity, respect, warmth, and friendliness (as HopeHealth measures with monthly client satisfaction surveys).

Based on their experiences running the HIV+ clinic and their assessment of the community health needs, the team outlined staffing objectives (by Year 2, they predicted, four medical providers and a staff of 16.7 FTEs would serve 3,750 users for 11.250 encounters); patient mix (at least 55% Medicaid with a Year 1 budget of $1.4 million, 63% of revenue coming from patient billing); and performance measures in terms of treating and preventing chronic disease, cancer, asthma, depression, and HIV. The following is an example of the performance measures and success goals they listed for one of these areas:

Diabetes

- Average HbA1c level for all patients with diabetes in last 12 months (Goal: <7%)
- Percentage of patients with 2 HbA1c tests in last 12 months (Goal: >90%)
- Percentage of patients with documented self-management goals in last 12 months (Goal: >70%)
- Percentage with blood pressure less than 130/80 in last 12 months (Goal: >40%)
- Percentage of pts with current prescription for aspirin or other antithrombotic agent (Goal: >80%)

The team wrapped up their definition of plan by describing the electronic data system the clinic would use to capture service data for continuous quality control.

Industry Analysis

Because the team's plan was dependent on successfully obtaining a community health center designation from the federal government, the team's industry analysis section describes the CHC history and characteristics, the current political climate for CHCs, the barriers to obtaining this designation, and the steps they had taken already to overcome some of these barriers. The CHC is described and compared with its "parallel" industry, the health care system:

Today there are 1,000 Community Health Centers that provide a medical home and family physician for 15 million people in every state and territory in the United States. About half of health center patients reside in rural areas. Nearly 40% of health center patients are uninsured.

CHCs differ from other health care providers in several key ways including:

- Being located in high-need areas as identified by the federal government; having elevated poverty and not enough physicians.
- Being open to all residents, regardless of insurance status.
- Providing free or reduced cost care based on ability to pay.
- Offering services that help their patients access health care, such as transportation, translation, case management, social work, health education, and home visitation.
- Governed by Boards where the majority of the members are patients (Federal regulation).

Successful health centers are those that find a way to balance the "safety net" ideal of the Economic Opportunity Act of 1964 with the need to increase income to deal with the rising costs of quality healthcare. It appears that uninsured patients cannot make up the majority of the patient mix. There must be a substantial Medicaid population and also some private insurance and Medicare patients.

Based on the history and characteristics of CHC they presented and analyzed, the team came up with their list of key success factors.

Once in the industry, the key success factors are four-fold:

- Create and maintain a system which ensures outpatient, ambulatory, primary care for anyone who needs it. Requires relationships with a network of vendors and contractors.
- Meet clinical quality standards consistently.
- Recruit and retain providers who reflect the target population or, at a minimum, are culturally competent.
- Maintain the proper balance between insured and uninsured clients for financial viability.

This industry analysis may seem different from what you are envisioning for your own. You may not be looking to the federal government or this type of "redefinition" of your organization. However, the steps involved may seem familiar in the general sense. Your goals are to (1) define and describe others who are addressing a need you want to fill; (2) show how you fit within the marketplace *and* are different (this team was different because there was no CHC in Florence, South Carolina); and (3) show that you know how to be successful in that industry.

Target Market

The team from Florence began their target market section with a quotation that you know was front and center of any visual aids they used to make their case:

> "I've had HIV for 10 years and I'm healthier than the rest of my family and most of my friends. We all live in the same neighborhood, but I'm the only one able to see a doctor. They might not have HIV, but they are a lot worse off then me. Why can't HopeHealth serve them, too?"
>
> > 41-year-old HIV+ African American woman
> > HopeHealth client
> > Consumer Advisory Committee, February 28, 2005

This quotation serves a few key purposes: one, it puts a human voice to their cause; two, it ends with a question that the reader can only answer with a ringing endorsement of serving the greater community; three, it endorses the care already being provided by HopeHealth ("I'm healthier than my friends"); and four, it reminds the reader that a committee made up of actual patients has gone in to the planning of this program (which is a requirement of CHCs). Who can argue with that?

The target market section goes on to describe inner city Florence in detail:

> Inner City Florence is comprised of a target population which is 98% African American. It is an area in which 32% of the people have an income below the poverty level, 14% are classified as severely poor, and almost half of the adults have no high school diploma. Other characteristics include:
>
> - 14.4% unemployment rate
> - 44% with no high school diploma (pop 25 yrs and older)
> - 26% of all housing units have no vehicle available
>
> The people of inner city Florence experience great health disparities. The target population death rate from hypertension is six times that of their white counterparts. The emergency department visit rate for diabetes is six times higher. The death rate from prostate cancer is 4.3 times higher and the case rate for HIV nine times higher than their white counterparts. Elevated hospitalization rates, emergency department visit rates, and health disparities also exist for heart disease, stroke, chronic obstructive pulmonary disease, breast cancer, all cancers, childhood asthma, and other conditions. There are very few options for the target population to receive needed primary care. Family practices are

not accepting new Medicaid patients and the local donation-funded "free" clinic has a long waiting list. This clinic indicates it can only meet 20% of the city's need.

This accumulation of data makes a compelling case for need. Note that the data points are specific, precise, and local.

Competition

This section contains a long list of local partners in the form of other health care providers, first responders, political personages, and community organizations as well as others interested but not yet committed to partnering. It also includes outright competitors of the proposed program. The list of partners is quite broad, including health care centers that want to ease the load on their emergency rooms, others who cannot serve Medicaid patients and want a place to which to refer them, a mental health center whose patients need a primary care home, and the police department that sees this program as a way to ameliorate some of the living conditions that cause inner city Florence to be a high crime area. The team had also had support from a powerful political figure in the state with connections to the state historic preservation office willing to help them secure space for the program in a historic building if necessary. Competitors include others providing care to this population in Florence, as well as a CHC about 30 miles away that might want to expand to inner city Florence.

As the team described in their industry analysis section, becoming a CHC is a political process that involves jumping through regulatory hoops: these would be classified as "barriers to entry." Indeed, some of the hoops are held by individuals and organizations that have an interest in keeping new organizations out of the industry. The team was smart to compile a long list of partners: fully nine entities were on board in support of the program when this plan was written, with another five interested in partnering, though not confirmed. What we can take away from this list is that, when community health is the goal, the list of potential partners is extremely broad.

Marketing Strategy

Planners decided to use the same name, slogan, and logo for the new CHC service as was being used for the HIV+ clinic. This was a strategic decision, not made without considering the negative associations patients might have with utilizing a clinic formerly only for HIV+ individuals. It was decided that any negative associations were outweighed by the positive reputation of the clinic in the community and among referring service providers. The business plan explained how HopeHealth would tailor its message according to the audience:

> Many patient referrals will come through formal arrangement or contracts. For example, we will very likely contract with Carolinas Medical Alliance to see their Medicaid patients. This contract could potentially equate to a couple thousand Medicaid patients. We will also forge formal referral agreements with the Emergency Departments of McLeod Regional Medical Center and Carolinas Hospital System. Mercy Medicine, the local "free" clinic prohibited from treating clients with Medicaid, has indicated they are in great need of a place to refer to.
>
> Therefore, HopeHealth will likely need to tailor its message based on the audience:
>
> 1. To providers, we want your excess Medicaid business.
> 2. To the Emergency Departments, we want your inappropriate and uninsured clientele.
> 3. To the community, we want you to come to us even if you don't have insurance.
> 4. To the community, we want you to come to us if you do have private insurance.

Recognizing the controversy of taking insured patients away from local health care providers, the team noted that message four might best be developed only after the project had been under way for several years.

Project Operations and Management

In this section, the team summarized the services it would provide and how they would be provided (whether on-site or through contracted services). They defined the target population, detailing the percentage of its patients they expected to get from different races, employment status and poverty level, educational achievement, gender, and age. They estimated the percentage of households that would not have a vehicle, which affects the clinic's transportation offerings, and listed the clinic hours of operations. Based on all this, they were able to detail management and staff needs and attached an organizational chart with explanations about authority and delegation channels. They listed the operational partners; the list of individuals and organizations with business relationships with the clinic number about 23 and include health care entities, laboratories, pharmacies, community groups, and transportation and other services. Finally, they outlined the organizational culture already in place at HopeHealth and briefly discussed how the new program might affect—and be affected by—the current culture.

Implementation Plan and Timeline

Some teams present this section in table form; others use a bar graph to show when different elements will be completed. This team presented their implementation plan and timeline by listing "completed-by" dates. They included stuff they had already done; for example:

Completed pre-September 2005
- Board voted to pursue community health center and new building
- Reviewed results from City of Florence Turning Point Initiative Forces of Change Assessment
- Conducted key informant interviews with patients, family members of patients, HopeHealth clinicians, case managers, and outreach staff.
- Conducted consumer focus groups
- Implemented survey for community health and human service providers
- Conducted staff and Board preparation activities (group meetings)
- Board received training from SCPHCA (called "Health Center Governance Boot Camp")
- Had several consultations with SCPHCA
- Met with Black River (competitor) and reviewed their affiliation proposal
- Met with CEO of Carolinas Hospital System to discuss support for new center and facility
- Met with COO of Carolinas Medical Alliance to discuss how proposed center would fit into the medical community and to solicit support
- Developed new "health center-compliant" by-laws for board ratification

Accounting for all the months up to implementation:

June 2006–September 2006
- Start providing services on day one of the CHC grant award. Begin by serving our existing 720 patients. Use existing staff and physicians initially.
- Send out press releases to television, print, and radio re: announcement of new community health center. Arrange for feature story in local newspaper.
- Recruit and hire appropriate staff.
- Purchase needed supplies and equipment. Order any needed wiring and networking.
- Order and install new billing and data collection software.
- Establish any new contracts or Memoranda of Agreement.

- Establish new policies and procedures as we anticipate/ encounter problems.
- Participate in mandated trainings or technical assistance.
- Evaluate likelihood of future success in September (the end of the four month start-up phase).
- Continue or exit the community health center service.
- If exit, determine another way or model to serve inner city Florence.

Note that the task list is specific and that it includes contingencies at various decision points.

Risks and Exit Plan

The team and Management Academy staff considered this plan a long shot. It is difficult to get CHC status. The federal government makes the process difficult because CHCs are able to bill the government significantly higher rates for the services they provide. In addition to the difficult selection process, the Florence team was worried about competition from other health care organizations, as well as risks due to increased liability, accountability to the government, political whims, and future needs to find new money streams.

The team did a very good job enumerating the risks of their proposal. They even outlined what they would do if they failed so completely (after getting funding) that the federal government asked them to pay back $100,000! In fact, they did such a good job explaining the risks and unknowns that after they presented the plan at the Management Academy, the team was nominated for the tongue-in-cheek "least likely to succeed" award. The lesson is that, in this case, seeing the potential risks was better than not seeing them.

Financials

Finance was a driver in the decision to write this plan, and analyzing the finances was a key function of the business plan for this team. Once designated a CHC, the clinic would be able to charge a Medicaid rate about three times what private physicians can charge. Based on their analysis, HopeHealth would only need grants for about one-third of its total funding as a CHC, compared with 95% without the CHC designation. As an existing care facility, HopeHealth could assume that the new center would start generating revenue immediately. The following lists assumptions for the first five years:

Revenue.
Year 1 Total: $1,372,091
$506,250 in grant revenue

$150 per patient × 3375 patients = $506,250

$865,841 in billing revenue

$125 per Medicaid visit × 5569 visits × 98% Collection Rate (CR) = $682,202

$125 per Medicaid mental health visit × 800 visits × 98% CR = $63,504

$80 per Medicare visit × 1094 visits × 95% CR = $83,144

$40 per private insurance visit × 810 visits × 80% CR = $25,920

Self-pay/Uninsured sliding scale = $11,071

Year 2 Total: $1,522,578
$562,500 in grant revenue

$150 per patient × 3750 patients = $562,500

$960,078 in billing revenue

$125 per Medicaid visit × 6188 visits × 98% Collection Rate (CR) = $758,030

$125 per Medicaid mental health visit × 800 visits × 98% CR = $63,504

$80 per Medicare visit × 1205 visits × 95% CR = $91,580

$40 per private insurance visit × 900 visits × 80% CR = $28,800

Self-pay/Uninsured sliding scale = $18,164

Year 3 Total: $1,667,488
$618,750 in grant revenue

$150 per patient × 4125 patients = $618,750

$1,048,738 in billing revenue

$125 per Medicaid visit × 6806 visits × 98% Collection Rate (CR) = $833,735

$125 per Medicaid mental health visit × 800 visits × 98% CR = $63,504

$80 per Medicare visit × 1318 visits × 95% CR = $100,168

$40 per private insurance visit × 1238 visits × 80% CR = $39,616

Self-pay/Uninsured sliding scale = $11,715

Year 4 Total: $1,828,612
$675,000 in grant revenue

$150 per patient × 4500 patients = $675,000

$1,153,612 in billing revenue

> Based on historical financial data from adding 375 patients per
> year for last three years. We can assume a 10% increase in billing
> revenue, given similar reimbursement rates and patient mix.

Year 5 Total: $2,000,223
$731,250 in grant revenue

$150 per patient × 4875 patients = $731,250

$1,268,973 in billing revenue

> Based on historical financial data from adding 375 patients per
> year for last four years. We can assume a 10% increase in billing
> revenue, given similar reimbursement rates and patient mix.

This team really grappled with the numbers. The section goes on
to list FTE totals, brief job descriptions, and salaries (rising over the
years) for all personnel, and calculates detailed expenses for travel,
equipment and supplies, contracted services, and space for the new
project. These are plugged into a complete five-year budget with revenue assumptions, and the break-even analysis wraps up the section.

Results

The team graduated from the Management Academy in April 2006 and
HopeHealth submitted their CHC application in December of that year.
The application required a grant proposal and a business plan, and po-
litical support in the form of backing from the South Carolina Primary
Health Care Association (SPHCA, or Association), which lobbies at the
federal level for CHCs and protects the interests of existing Centers.

The two HopeHealth team members working on this project were
the organization's Director of Development and QI, who was mainly
responsible for writing the grant proposal, and the Executive Director,
who worked behind the scenes to secure the support of the Association
and other key partners. The business plan written at the Management
Academy did not change significantly between April and December.

The process was very competitive. There had been no new CHCs
in South Carolina for eight years; there were already 19 in the state and
only 1,000 in the whole United States. The Association limits who
they support not only because the members of that organization are

the directors of other CHCs in the state (and thus potential competitors with any new Centers), but also because the Association needs to protect the reputation of all its Center members by ensuring that only strong, legitimate contenders get the designation. The HopeHealth Executive Director joined that board, developed strong relationships with its members, and eventually gained their support.

The HopeHealth team also had to get the support of their own board for the project. The idea had been discussed for years. In fact, before attending the Management Academy, the HopeHealth members had begun creating an application, only to have that year's program cancelled because of Hurricane Katrina, three days before the grant was due. The challenge was to convince the board that broadening the patient mix would not undermine the original mission. The executive director argued that being a CHC would actually strengthen the HIV+ program over time because HIV funding was drying up. Rather than establish a waiting list or cut services, the new designation would allow care for HIV+ patients to be covered by the new funding as well.

The application with grant proposal and business plan was submitted December 6, 2006. In June, the team was informed that they had received a score of 94 on the application, a very high mark.

They were in business!

Implementing the Plan

The CHC grant allows for a four-month phase-in time, but one of the HopeHealth team's selling points had been that they were equipped to start operations right away. Which they did. By July 1, 2007, they were accepting patients. They hadn't advertised, but news of the new program had spread, and articles had been published in local papers about the program in its planning stages. The Management Academy always publishes press releases in the local papers of teams who win blue ribbons at the Management Academy graduation (a high honor given to only one team per cohort, indicating that staff believe that the plan has great potential). As of this writing (less than a month into implementation), already a couple dozen patients have been seen or scheduled to be seen at the newly designated community health center.

The HopeHealth press release, incidentally, got the attention of a board member from the local free clinic who initially argued that HopeHealth would be taking her clinic's business away. The free clinic organization actually submitted a newspaper article on their own behalf shortly afterward. Rather than fight a war of words, though, the HopeHealth management opened up a conversation with a potential competitor, and that competitor became a supporter when they realized that HopeHealth and the free clinic would be referring patients to each other, due to their differing admissions policies and treatment options.

The policy of building relationships has served the Clinic program implementation well in many ways. The Clinic started serving patients quickly in part because they were able to hire a full-time physician. Previously, the work of the HIV+ clinic was done by part-time contracted physicians. This seemed a big leap from its beginnings in 1991 as a home-based support group for people with HIV and their families, but now the organization needed to leap even further and convince a physician to make HopeHealth his or her primary clinical home. Several advisors and colleagues estimated it would take them a full year to recruit a physician to move to Florence and begin work. The local hospital shared ideas and allowed their recruiter to coach them on the recruitment process, all the while warning that it would be several months before they got even a nibble for the position. However, through connections at a local private practice group of infectious disease physicians who contract to work in the HIV+ clinic, HopeHealth learned about a new infectious disease physician moving to Florence from New York; his wife was also a physician in need of work. This family practice physician, comfortable and experienced with all age groups, was a perfect fit for HopeHealth and has been a critical addition to the team.

The Clinic is still relying on word of mouth for business, because much needs to be done to bring it completely up to speed. Specifically, the fiscal and information systems must be put in place before volume gets too high, and the board membership must be changed to fit the federal regulations. Processes for moving forward in these areas are in place.

Discussion

We chose this case study for several reasons. It is an implemented project that's fairly recent and clearly fits the Management Academy model in terms of revenue generation, partnership, and entrepreneurial spirit. We actually liked the fact that very few readers of this book will ever find themselves applying to become a community health center—we want for this to be an example, not a template.

Finally, this plan seems to highlight many of the messages we have tried to weave through this book. The HopeHealth business plan started from two inextricably related necessities: mission—serve the community—and money—diversify funding sources in order to survive. The team hadn't written a business plan before. One of them had been told "you will never run a community health center." Maybe you have never written a business plan before. The message we want to leave you with about business planning is this: you can do it, and you should.

In situations like yours, others have written business plans, have learned from the experience, and have found that their business plan helped them implement a project. In some cases they implemented a project they might never have considered, or would never have constructed in the way they did. In many cases—as with HopeHealth— the business plan facilitated or added on to a grant application. In some cases—as with HopeHealth—the business plan team included governmental and nonprofit members, and the business plan ultimately served the needs of both.

HopeHealth had to write a business plan—a business plan is a requirement to become a CHC. Their decision to become a CHC, though, was their own, and that decision was driven by exactly the sort of analysis we have put forward in this book. HopeHealth was an organization almost entirely dependent on HIV grant funding. Now they enjoy a much more diverse funding stream, which in turn allows them to pursue their mission more effectively, now and into the future.

HopeHealth will continue to face challenges. No business plan accounts for every eventuality. Their approach will continue to evolve. Business planning is a habit of mind: the plan is a process, a way of thinking about a problem and attacking it. And that process is repeatable.

Chapter 15

Creating *Your* Public Health Business Plan

W e've seen lots of business plans over the years. As of this writing, we've run 21 sessions of the Management Academy, with an average of 12 teams per session: that's about 250 business plans. We've informally tracked teams throughout that time, and formally surveyed and interviewed teams from the first six years of the Academy about their business plan outcomes. In this final chapter of *Public Health Business Planning*, we will share some of our lessons learned about which plans become successful, sustained programs.

First a caveat: business plan implementation is not the primary goal of the Management Academy for Public Health program. We assign business plans as an educational tool to help managers practice new skills. Indeed, a few teams over the years have treated the business plan as purely an academic exercise. But virtually all teams make their plans "real-life" (even those few who see it ultimately as an exercise) and most do intend to implement their plans. At graduation, 85% of our graduates report that they intend to implement the plan on which they have spent the previous nine months.

Still, based on our research, only about one third of that "intend to implement" group will be successful: just under 30% of the teams. Why?

The Value of "Failure"

Let's start with the success rate in the private sector. It is very close to the success rate for the plans we see. Generally in the private sector, the rule of thumb is that only 10% of new initiatives will be really successful. Another 20% will get implemented, but will earn only enough to subsist; they will struggle along. That leaves 70% as failures. Business plans often fail. This makes sense if you think about it: if business planning were easy, there wouldn't be nearly as many business planning books on the market.

In the risk-averse worlds you inhabit—both health care and government are generally very risk-averse—a 70% failure rate may look scary. Luckily we're talking about ideas, not clinical outcomes. As an entrepreneur, your number of failures builds your chances for success. This is the "nothing ventured, nothing gained" principle in action. Companies that depend on innovation for growth—3M is a classic example in business schools—often use number of failures as a benchmark. If you have many failures, it indicates that many ideas are getting tested. People who study innovation boil down the lesson this way: "fail forward faster." Failures are learning experiences; use them scientifically to move forward to the right answer.

Our students live this lesson every year. It isn't unusual for a team to go through three business plan ideas in the first week of the Management Academy. It isn't at all unusual for teams to abandon an idea after doing a feasibility plan and start over. Those "failed" ideas often help the team move on to a better, more robust idea in the end. Far worse is to be on the team that sticks with their initial idea, writes a full business plan, and only later discovers that it can't work.

If your feasibility plan convinces you to abandon an idea that isn't likely to work, you just failed forward. You eliminated an idea with a low probability of success—and probably learned something about a specific barrier or two. Your next idea will adapt to that barrier and raise your probability of success.

What Can Go *Right* in Public Health Business Planning?

We've talked a lot in this book about what can go wrong in public health business planning. Luckily, though many plans fail, some succeed, and we know a lot about what can go right in this process. We've gleaned the following success factors from our experiences working with public health teams, from our outcomes evaluation work including surveys and interviews, and from developing case studies based on the outcomes of several teams. Many of these factors mutually support each other.

Writing a really good business plan seems to help. It isn't a decisive factor, however; some plans look good on paper but don't actually get implemented. Others look risky on paper but turn out to be great. Of course in some instances, as in the HopeHealth Community Health Clinic we talked about in Chapter 14, the business plan is a required part of a grant application. And other Management Academy graduates have told us that learning how to write the business plan (and doing it over and over) has just made them better at a lot of the things they have to do—assessing, partnering, figuring the finances, and so forth. Writing the business plan is a way of forcing you to think about other things that tend to turn out to be key factors for success. For example,

1. Committed Partners:

Many successful plans get that way by including partners from the community and integrating them tightly into the project. This could be because tighter integration typically means that the team has more information from a broader network in planning. The broader network can help build more buy-in, and political support can drive implementation. And plans with integrated partners are generally better for public health.

2. Hard Work:

We've found that teams that meet more often, do more research, make more site visits, and spend more time writing drafts seem to have better results. Talent is nice to have, but hard work really adds up. Over the course of a long, complicated process like business planning, bet on hard work.

A couple of factors seem to be hard-work multipliers: like pulleys that allow you to lift more. Teams that are committed to a common goal and have a good process for working together get more out of their hard work. Note how this factor works together with the "committed partners" factor: excited partners put energy into the system. Implemented plans typically have at least one passionate, energetic person that keeps the team on track. And as you've probably figured out by now, writing a good business plan in itself requires hard work and dedication.

3. Support in the Organization:

According to our research the primary reason that business planners fail to implement in public health settings is lack of organizational support. In some cases, organizations are finding flaws in plans that the planners thought were fine. You have some control over this outcome: share your ideas early with staff and decision makers to uncover barriers. If you understand the flaws that your decision makers see, in time you can address them. In return, decision makers will support your work.

In some cases, though, organizations fail to support entrepreneurial ideas simply because organizations resist change. For some of you, the ideas in this book represent change. Every year at the Management Academy we have teams that say, "No way can we get our organization to do things this way." And they at least had the support of their bosses to attend the program! You may not even have that base level of support for trying new things. Success—that is, implementation—requires you to find a strategy that will help decision makers get past the risk. Find a low-risk way to test your plan before roll-out; design the plan to be easily reversible; start the plan small and phase it in over time. Ideally you have a whole team that can help push—including committed partners. Do find champions in the organization who understand your vision and will push with you.

4. Lots of Practice:

You learn music by practicing an instrument. You learn business planning by planning businesses. Our research supports this simple notion. Teams that fail to implement one plan often go on to develop and implement other revenue-generating plans. Our recent research found that half of our "failed to implement" group had gone on to implement another business plan. They failed forward. This factor clearly connects with hard work: the more you work at business planning, the better results you are liable to get. It might also connect with organizational support issues: it might take more examples to convince your decision makers.

So your organization does not seem to want entrepreneurial ideas. That does not mean your organization does not need them and will not value them once you implement them. Keep trying it. Failure that contains learning is a common precursor to success. Success will lead to more success—because most organizations do learn. Implement one revenue-generating plan and see what happens in your organization.

It's Your Turn

You've read the book and begun thinking about the feasibility of your project. You've read a lot of examples from successful (and unsuccessful) teams. Once you've done your homework, your plan will be half done! Your homework begins with the question templates at the end of each chapter. As we said way back in Chapter 1, the templates in this book serve to help you begin work on every business plan section and to break the whole down into manageable chunks. At an altogether different—and equally important—level, these templates serve the same function that the diploma serves for the scarecrow in the *Wizard of Oz*: they give you the confidence to believe in your own abilities. Business planning in public health is possible, if you believe. Don't sell the Wizard short: you really are doing something slightly magical. Business planning is about much more than filling out templates, doing math to find break-even, or gathering demographics data. You do those things as ways to help you predict the future—and change it, for the better.

We wish you luck and inspiration, support from your colleagues and superiors, a favorable economic climate, and no shortage of interested and able partners. Add these to your hard work and you can't fail. To see an ever-growing set of examples of innovative and successful public health business plans, or for information about how to become a Management Academy team, visit the Management Academy website at http://www.maph.unc.edu.

Afterword

From the Top Down: What a Leader Can Do

The model presented in *Public Health Business Planning: A Practical Guide* is a powerful way to think about supporting programs and services you might otherwise not be able to provide to your constituents. Ideally, these programs and services are part of a larger strategy for success that guides your organization from the top down. Leaders can help ensure success at individual, programmatic, and organizational levels through *empowering* and *enabling* their workforce to do the work they need to do.

Empowerment involves giving people the strength, dynamism, authority—i.e., the power—to do what they need to do. A leader empowers others by communicating the organization's vision so that it can be *seen* by others. Workers must be able to envision the goals they are working toward, which means they must first know what they are and then understand what they will look like. What will success at this new enterprise look like? Will it be a room crowded with people eager to purchase your services or products? Will it be a financial award from a federal agency? Will it be a book, long planned, finally published, and educating millions about business planning in public health? As a leader, it is important to know what success, at all levels, will look like and communicate that vision to your team.

If you communicate the vision well, you've gone a long way toward motivating your employees. Motivation also involves taking away the barriers to meeting the goals you've helped them envision. Often those barriers include negative energy, pessimism, and a lack of hope or expectation that the organization or individuals within the organization will reach those goals. A leader has to provide optimism and hope.

He or she also has to make that optimism meaningful—that is, realistic—to his or her employees. If you as a leader are working to build relationships with others in the community and in the political, business, and other realms, your employees' optimism about building partnerships for individual projects is more realistic. If you advocate for public health among a broad constituency, their optimism about getting the support they need may increase. If you actively support their efforts to apply new ways of thinking to old problems, they will attempt to achieve the goals that will fulfill the organization's long-term plan. Enabling employees with the tools to act, including skills development and training activities, personal development instruments, educational materials, and other resources, will also affect their optimism and efficacy. If you nurture an atmosphere of optimism and work to further the goals of your employees, they will succeed.

However at the same time that you're creating vision and positive energy among your staff, you must also express concrete, specific expectations. Hope is good. By expressing open-ended desires and hopes to your staff you give them idealistic aspirations to reach for. But if you don't also express your tangible, explicit expectations of them, they will not only not reach for your aspirations, they won't even know what they are.

This last point gets to the differences—and the necessary interrelationship—between leadership and management. Our society glorifies leadership, and indeed it is important to have inspiring, visionary leaders. But without good management translating that vision into concrete steps and expectations, nothing will actually get done.

Edward L. Baker, Jr., MD, MPH
Director, North Carolina Institute for Public Health

Index

Page numbers followed by t or f indicate tables or figures, respectively. Numbers followed by "n" indicate endnotes.